RIDE THE RIGHT HORSE

Ride the Right Horse

Understanding the Core Equine Personalities & How to Work with Them

Yvonne Barteau

FOREWORD BY CAROL LAVELL

Storey Publishing

*The mission of Storey Publishing is to serve our customers by
publishing practical information that encourages
personal independence in harmony with the environment.*

Edited by Deborah Burns
Art direction and cover design by Cynthia McFarland
Text design by Jen Rork and Jessica Armstrong
Text production by Jessica Armstrong
Cover photographs by Erika Walsh
Interior photography by: courtesy of Arabian Nights Dinner Theater: 69; Jamie
  Barteau: 55; Kim Barteau: 91; Yvonne Barteau: 166; L.A. Photo Works: 25;
  © Bob Langrish: vii, xi; ©Terri Miller: 72, 75; Mary Phelps: 100; Tom Tanner:
  80; Bob Tarr: 10, 59; Erika Walsh: ii, 41, 132; Jody Woodruff: 63, 162
Illustrations by Jo Anna Rissanen
Indexed by Susan Olason, Indexes & Knowledge Maps

Printed in the United States by Versa Press
10 9 8 7 6 5 4 3 2 1

Library of Congress Cataloging-in-Publication Data

Barteau, Yvonne.
  Ride the right horse / by Yvonne Barteau.
    p. cm.
  Includes index.
  ISBN-13: 978-1-58017-662-0 (hardcover jacketed : alk. paper)
  1. Horses—Behavior. 2. Human-animal communication. 3. Horsemanship.
  I. Title.
SF281.B36 2007
636.1—dc22

                                                          2007001579

For all of the horses
who have helped define me.

CONTENTS

PART ONE: *Equine Temperament*

PART TWO: *The Four Horse Personality Types*

PART THREE: *Mixed Personalities*

PART FOUR: *You & Your Horse*

ACKNOWLEDGMENTS

This book would never have found print if it weren't for Deb Burns and all of the staff at Storey, who patiently and articulately made sense and structure out of my ideas and procedures. For that I am grateful.

I'd like also to express thanks to:

Bob Oury, whose horses enticed us to leave Florida, and who is the hardest-working man I know.

Gail Rodecker, my true "F" friend and Myers-Briggs consultant, who gave much of her time and insights to the personality segment of this book.

My husband and business partner, Kim, who is indeed a "gentleman in all weather and a smart and charming companion." We have become two sides of the same coin.

My children, Jamie, Jessica, Kassie, and Hudi. Being your mother gives me great pride and a never-ending sense of accomplishment.

Endel Ots, who is both friend and family to me. And to his father, Dr. Max Ots, for raising such a fine young man.

Ginna Frantz, who has believed in my riding and writing all along and supported me generously.

Erika Walsh, who redefines the word "busy" on a daily basis but still finds time to help me immensely.

Finally, I am forever indebted to the hundreds of horses who tolerated my ignorance as I learned to ride and who shaped my path by responding to me anyway. I have acquired more information from the horses in my life than I have from any other source and for that I am both grateful and humbled.

FOREWORD

YVONNE BARTEAU CAME INTO MY LIFE as a pupil in a dressage training session. Surrounded by a herd of horses at various levels, she was clearly an ardent competitor — even reciting from memory twenty-one dressage tests!

At one dressage show I saw her jumping from one horse to the next with barely enough time to warm up. I made the comment that horses were not cars, and that she needed to take more ride-in time to account for their individuality. Now comes the book!

- -

Horses are Yvonne's teachers.

In this book she teaches the trainer how to learn

from the horses, and how to understand their different

personalities. It's all about how to have

a relationship with them.

- -

A trainer may well be born not made, but Yvonne's knowledge is from the proverbial school of hard knocks. And speaking of schools, what's in this book is not taught in any school. The reader gets a heavy dose of reality. Well-organized information is delivered first with a description of a horse's personality, followed by the entertainment: real case examples.

*Carol Lavell and Gifted at the 1992 Olympic Games in Barcelona,
Spain, where they won a Team Bronze medal in dressage.*

Yes, horses are Yvonne's teachers, but she takes one step beyond. In this book she teaches the trainer how to learn from the horses, and how to understand their different personalities. It's all about how to have a relationship with them.

Yvonne writes with a huge depth of perception, and she is armed with a vast array of experiences. You will not find another book like this one.

— CAROL LAVELL

International FEI competitor, Olympic medalist

PREFACE

Have you ever wondered what goes on inside a horse's head? More specifically, how individual horses might view the world around them? That idea seized me as a horse-crazy ten-year-old and has yet to let go. I studied, read, and reread my meager collection of horse stories, wondering if all horses were like Black Beauty, Flicka, and The Pie. Or were they as different from one another as I was from my own brothers and sister? I speculated the latter to be true long before I had access to any "real" subjects.

Decades have passed since then. I am now a successful dressage trainer, and my childhood passion has led me through a lifetime of studying and learning all that I could about my favorite creature, the horse. My best and most reliable information has always come directly from the noble steeds themselves. I still remember, and am grateful to, those early lesson ponies in Canada and the racehorses I met and studied with on a five-year learning expedition around the Standardbred and Thoroughbred racetracks of America. These new friendships included some flighty, volatile, and at times unpredictable young racehorses.

By my late twenties I had developed a reputation for redeeming unrideable and ill-tempered "rogues" — misunderstood and confused mounts unable to tolerate human ignorance any longer. I then furthered my own education by joining the Arabian Nights Dinner Theater, where I was exposed to sixty-seven equine dinner theatre performers. In the last ten years my journey has led me into the world of imported and domestic warmbloods. As an FEI trainer and competitor, based at Indian Hills Training Center in Illinois, I now work with the horses most suited to participate in the ever-growing sport of dressage.

A few years ago my husband, Kim, who (blessedly for me) has also been training horses for his entire life, and I started discussing the very real differences in equine personalities. We began to articulate something we had known subconsciously for years: that how a horse will react to any situation is grounded in his basic personality, in addition to his either instinctive or conditioned response to stimuli. Although most horses have the same natural instincts, they do not share the same training or personality traits.

Kim and I had both amassed years of experience on the training side, but the personality part was still undefined. Together we began to categorize which behaviors and characteristics a horse might display that would help us define his individual personality type. Fortunately, our combined experiences had given us many hundreds of subjects, horses we remembered well enough to accurately describe their basic, recurring preferences.

Long hours of conversation followed, with a few trusted peers, about how many different personality types there actually were. We concluded that there are four basic categories of personality — Social, Fearful, Aloof, and Challenging — with many horses sharing traits from two different types. We also determined that, unlike people who are either introverted or extroverted, horses were either passive or aggressive in how they displayed their personality traits. Significantly, each type of personality has its own strengths and weaknesses in regard to trainability.

Of course, many factors can influence a horse's behavior. The personality and behaviors of the broodmare can have at least a short-term effect on some foals. Imprinting, or lack of it, has a decided effect on some personality types and less on others. Consistent, fair handling from birth on will make a definite impact on the future behavior of almost all personality types. Nevertheless, if four different personality types were handled the same way by the same trainer with the same expectations, each individual's personality type would remain his most discernible or defining feature to any sensitive horseman.

In this day and age, there are many competent trainers and an ever-increasing number of talented horses in any discipline. The dynamics of each horse's fundamental personality, coupled with that of his most frequent rider, trainer, and/or handler, can be enough to create a winning or losing combination. This book is designed to put words to the thoughts that knowledgeable horsemen and horsewomen around the world already share. A horse's basic personality, along with the environmental influences he is exposed to, dictates the way he might approach any given situation, be it a training day, a competition, or a visitor in his own field at home.

Why Read This Book?

Why do you need to know what type of personality your horse (or any horse) might possess? The best and simplest answer is that comprehending some fundamentals about the basic temperament and personality of the horse leads to clearer understanding of his behavior patterns and thus an increased ability to handle and influence him.

Knowledge about equine temperaments should not take the place of understanding conformation, gaits, and training issues when evaluating a horse. Personality should always be thought of "in addition to" and not "instead of," in order to give prospective owners and riders a clearer picture of the whole horse. Yet it is proven that horses of different temperaments respond much better when they are handled and trained by someone who understands their basic personality and has sound and safe training strategies and procedures that enhance this understanding.

Horses are wonderful creatures, but they are not human. They are herd animals that respond at times instinctively to certain circumstances or stimuli. Because their basic personality influences how they might respond to a variety of situations, understanding the differences in how the four different types react and relate to their world will help you, the rider, make correct choices in dealing with them.

Until this time there has been very little written information available to riders without years of experience or many hundreds of subjects to study. Most trainers and "horse whisperers" make everyday use of their own insights and knowledge about horse personalities even if they might use different words to describe them. Understanding the temperament of the horse is what sets true horsemen apart from the rest of the riders and horse enthusiasts that make up the horse world. I hope that this book will prompt you to look at all of your equine friends with a more educated and empathetic eye.

PART ONE

EQUINE TEMPERAMENT

An overview of the four horse personality types and their passive and aggressive variations

Horses sort human

and equine temperament instinctively

and without prejudice, an ability that often

enables them to see us more clearly than

we see ourselves.

CHAPTER ONE

THE FOUR HORSE PERSONALITIES

PICTURE YOURSELF IN A FIELD with a number of mares and foals. You are a stranger to this particular group of horses. After taking off your jacket and hanging it on a fence post, you step away from the fence and spend a few minutes quietly observing the scene in front of you.

Three of the youngsters have already spotted you. One has retreated to the far side of her mother, where she cautiously watches you from under the mare's belly. Another, who appeared both interested and alert at your arrival, is making his way determinedly toward your jacket. Upon reaching it he wastes no time before mouthing it, grabbing it, pulling it off the fence, and happily shaking it around. Another youngster stands at some distance from her mother. She has not moved much at all since you first appeared; in fact she seems neither interested in nor intimidated by any of the proceedings. The last of the group, with all the swagger of a school-yard bully, rushes in to grab and then argue about who should keep the jacket.

You have just witnessed the four personality types of horses — Fearful, Social, Aloof, and Challenging — all clearly observable before the foals are even weaned! Of course, environment and life experiences, not to mention handling and training, will play a large part in shaping these youngsters, but their innate personalities (especially the "louder" ones) will remain observable to anyone who takes the time to study them. We will discuss this topic much more fully later in this book.

The following pages list the four basic personality groups and the characteristics that best define each. As described in chapter 2, the way an individual horse might display any of these characteristics can range from passive (not so easy to detect) to aggressive (very easy to recognize) and various stages in between.

Whatever personality type your horse is,

almost all horses can be trained productively and effectively,

depending on your intended use.

You may recognize your horse somewhere among these descriptions. Many horses have personality characteristics of two different groups, which makes them slightly more complex individuals. We will discuss these mixed personalities later on. If your horse seems difficult to read, he may be more passive (quiet) about his personality traits. If his personality seems larger than life (very loud), he is probably more aggressive about his personality type.

Whatever personality type your horse is, and wherever he ends up on the aggressivity scale, almost all horses can be trained productively and effectively, depending on your intended use. Some types, however, will require a more skilled rider or many hours of schooling with an experienced trainer.

Social Characteristics

▶ **Interaction.** Want to observe and interact with the world.

▶ **Need for personal space.** Tolerant of people or other horses in their personal space. Appear almost welcoming.

▶ **Relationship to herd/humans.** Rarely at the top of the pecking order but often second or friend to the chief.

▶ **Vocalizing.** Often more vocal than other personality types.

▶ **Adaptability.** Generally accepting of new experiences.

▶ **Reactiveness.** Generally tend to underreact to a new stimulus; not usually explosive.

▶ **Attention span.** Attention span can be very short, especially in youngsters. May have trouble focusing on one thing in a busy environment. May leave own feed bucket to socialize.

▶ **Weaning.** More confident, less worried and panicky, at weaning time than most other foals.

▶ **Response to training.** Once trained are usually steady performers; will need occasional tune-ups on basic issues.

▶ **Lessons & routine.** Appreciate variety in their lessons.

▶ **Tolerance.** Tend to be more tolerant of inept or poor handling than other types.

▶ **Happiest & most content** when allowed to interact with other horses, people, and the environment.

Fearful Characteristics

▶ **Interaction.** Guarded or cautious (especially as youngsters).

▶ **Need for personal space.** May indicate a need for more personal space than they have; may be somewhat claustrophobic when uncomfortable or confined.

▶ **Relationship to herd/humans.** Very dependent on social structure. Likely to bond with another horse or human.

▶ **Vocalizing.** Usually vocalize out of anxiety or loneliness, and upon the arrival, with or without food, of someone they have bonded with.

▶ **Adaptability.** Not immediately at ease in new situations.

▶ **Reactiveness.** May have strong, quick, or reflexive-type reactions to stimuli or aids. Almost overreactive.

▶ **Fight or flight?** More flight- than fight-oriented.

▶ **Behavior quirks.** May be poor eaters; may be stall walkers.

▶ **Attention span.** Once comfortable, often have a long attention span.

▶ **Weaning.** May be insecure and panicky at weaning time.

▶ **Response to training.** Once trained, usually make very strong efforts to comply.

▶ **Lessons & routine.** Prefer consistent, predictable routines; have trouble adjusting to multiple riders.

- **Tolerance of poor handling.** Not tolerant of poor treatment.

- **Happiest & most content** when in the reassuring presence of a stronger personality, either human or equine.

Aloof Characteristics

- **Interaction.** Not particularly interactive in herd situations.

- **Need for personal space.** Tolerate, but don't always welcome, intrusion in their personal space.

- **Relationship to herd/humans.** May appear somewhat independent of both horses and people.

- **Behavior quirks.** May exhibit disassociative-type behavior, such as cribbing or weaving.

- **Response to aids.** Often seem to have a delayed reaction — sometimes strong, sometimes very slight — to stimuli or aids. Reaction time is slower than in other types. Will often appear to deliberately shut out all sources of stimulation, including rider aids.

- **Reactiveness.** Generally not prone to explosive behaviors; show natural restraint.

- **Response to training.** Once trained will need occasional reality checks.

- **Happiest & most content** when allowed ample "alone time."

Challenging Characteristics

▶ **Interaction.** Strong sense of self: may seem prideful or arrogant. Stallions generally more aggressive than stallions of other types.

▶ **Need for personal space.** Guarded or somewhat territorial about their personal space. Must be taught quite early not to invade their handlers' personal space.

▶ **Relationship to herd/humans.** Usually near the top of the pecking order in the herd. Need constant clarification of their place in the social order of the horse-trainer relationship.

▶ **Adaptability.** Initially resistant to new suggestions.

▶ **Reactiveness.** Prone to more explosive reactions.

▶ **Response to aids.** Confrontational about stimuli or aids.

▶ **Fight or flight?** More fight than flight tendencies.

▶ **Behavior quirks.** When young, and even into adulthood, may exhibit threatening behavior such as biting, kicking, charging, or rushing.

▶ **Opportunism.** Quickly spot and exploit opportunities provided by timid or inexperienced riders.

▶ **Response to training.** When properly trained make reliable, confident partners.

▶ **Often strong, brave performers** with true charisma.

▶ **Happiest & most content** when having their own way.

Why Personality Matters

Horses can be as different from each other as people are, and like people, some horses require more time, knowledge, and/or experience to get through to. A basic understanding of equine personalities will help you recognize and respect the variations among the four types. This knowledge will lead you toward fairer and more empathetic treatment and riding of your horse.

These insights will also alert you to the personality types that require more skillful handling. Certain personalities may never be easy or appropriate for amateurs or beginner riders without the benefit of knowledgeable, consistent help. It is far better to be aware of these potential incompatibilities before you acquire such a horse.

- -

Certain personalities may never be appropriate for

beginner riders without knowledgeable, consistent help.

- -

Years ago, as a younger and much more ignorant horseman, I managed to be successful with some difficult types without getting hurt in the process. Later, after gaining much-needed experience and information, I realized how lucky I had been to avoid serious injury. As a general guideline, however, it is unwise to rely on luck to see you through potentially dangerous situations with horses. Information, experience, and the right kind of help remain the safest and smartest route to success.

*My husband, Kim, and I often study horses, as here
at a show in Indiana.*

Learning to Look at Horses

It is always best to know as much as possible about the basic personality of a horse before you consider buying him. If you already own
a horse, interacting with him every day provides information that
will help you handle and train him appropriately according to his
individual personality type. Once you have learned the traits of the
four types, the process of identifying temperament in any given
horse becomes much more streamlined.

It may seem difficult when you first study a new horse and
attempt to determine his personality traits in a rational fashion.
Keep these suggestions in mind.

- **Stay open-minded.** You will make mistakes of judgment in your early stages and this is to be expected.

- **Never stop gathering information.** Keen observation of your horse's actions and interactions is the true key to success.

- **Don't give up!** Objective observation skills are valuable for any horse enthusiast and can be developed only through practice. Familiarity with temperament type is a useful tool for any equine endeavor.

When you first attempt to classify any horse by character you must pay close attention to both his actions and his interactions with his environment, people (both new and familiar), and other horses. These observations will help you to categorize your subject horse as fearful, aloof, social, or challenging. Once that is determined you must examine your horse's behavior even more closely to decide whether he is either passive or aggressive about displaying his individual characteristics.

Some horses, however, will define themselves as being very loud (aggressive) or very quiet (passive) before you can even observe enough behavior to determine which of the four personality groups they fit into. There is no exact order of insights. I may see a noisy boisterous horse attracting much attention to himself at a horse show, and my first impression is wow, there is a fairly aggressive "something." Usually such behavior will encourage me to study the horse for a few minutes, and I will often go over and talk to the trainer or owner and ask her a few questions just to see what type of horse he is.

Determining type is a skill that is not unlike any other, such as analyzing gaits, breeding, or conformation. The right information, lots of practice, and the ability to set preconceived notions aside and remain observant at all times: these ingredients make for success in determining temperament on any horse.

BREEDS & PERSONALITY

In the introduction to the personality profiles beginning in chapter 3, I have listed some breeds that may be associated with a certain personality type. I have listed only the breeds where the majority of horses my husband and I studied fell into that personality group or a mix of that group. This does not mean to imply that every Quarter Horse will be an aloof type or that every Dutch Warmblood will be of social character. You may still find fearful and social Quarter Horses or challenging Dutch Warmbloods, so studying each horse as an individual before guessing at his personality type will always remain paramount.

CHAPTER TWO

PASSIVE & AGGRESSIVE VARIATIONS

WHEN YOU ACQUIRE A NEW HORSE, in addition to learning whether he is social, fearful, aloof, or challenging, it is equally important to determine if he is passive or aggressive in expressing his temperament. The difference between the passive and aggressive variations within any given personality type can be quite significant and could be the defining factor in whether you will be able to have a productive relationship with a certain personality at all. As a general rule, the more passive a horse is (quiet about displaying his personality traits) in any of the four personality types (social, fearful, aloof, or challenging), the easier he will be to handle.

I picture the aggressivity range as a sliding scale with numbers attached to it. I might assign very passive horses a 1, 2, or 3, and moderately passive horses 4 through 7. An 8 or above would indicate aggressive or very loud personality traits.

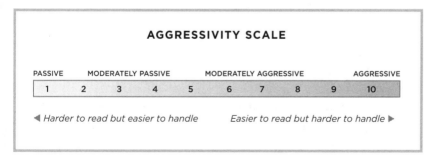

AGGRESSIVITY SCALE

PASSIVE	MODERATELY PASSIVE		MODERATELY AGGRESSIVE		AGGRESSIVE
1	2	3	4	5	6	7	8	9	10

◀ *Harder to read but easier to handle*   *Easier to read but harder to handle* ▶

The only way to determine where your subject horse is on the aggressivity scale is by studying his behavior closely, sometimes during multiple or lengthy observations. Your subject horse may be one you have owned for some time, one you are considering for purchase, or one of the lesson horses at your local stable. It is helpful if you have experienced or can study other horses to which you can compare your subject's behavior.

SOCIAL RANGE: Contented to Boisterous

Picture, if you will, two horses that would both be described as having social personality traits, yet they behave very differently from each other. The first, a quietly passive-social gelding, is just interested and interactive enough to get his job done each day. The second is his aggressively social counterpart. Instead of quiet, cool, and low-key, you have a distracted and distractible individual, interested in everything and anyone, a fun-loving horse who is intent on living life to the fullest. The passive horse's personality, while still social, is like a radio with the volume turned down so low that you can barely hear it. The aggressively social horse has the same personality traits, but the volume may be so loud that these same qualities may seem almost intrusive or annoying.

To some people, a loud, boisterous horse might seem fun and interactive, but to a quiet person or a more unskilled one without a lot of time to commit, an aggressively social horse might be too much to handle. This is why it is essential to identify the passive-aggressive variation of each type in addition to the type itself. The two case studies that follow will compare an aggressively social horse and a passively social horse in order to highlight these differences.

Here is how a horse's aggressivity can affect the personality traits of the social horse, introduced in chapter 1.

▶ **Interaction.** More passively social horses are content to observe; more aggressive ones will want to interact.

▶ **Need for personal space.** More passively social types are tolerant and welcoming, while more aggressively social horses will be happy to invade your personal space.

▶ **Vocalizing.** More passive horses are usually quieter than their more aggressive counterparts.

▶ **Adaptability.** Passive or aggressive equally accepting.

▶ **Attention span.** The more aggressive your social horse is, the more easily distracted he will be, even after some training. He may leave his own feed bucket to socialize.

▶ **Weaning.** Whether passive or aggressive, more confident at weaning time than most other foals.

▶ **Response to training.** The more aggressive types will need refresher courses more often than the more passive types.

▶ **Lessons & routine.** Passive types need less variety and stimulation than do their more aggressive counterparts.

▶ **Tolerance.** Passively social types tolerate inept handling better than any other type. Aggressively social horses will require a little more skill to handle.

EXAMPLE: *Bad Joke (aggressively social)*

My younger brother, Spencer, came to stay with me for a time when I worked on the racetrack. He was not a skilled horse handler. He had participated in a few forays around a field on a trail horse when he was a kid, but in his opinion horses were a poor substitute for a dirt bike. Spencer knew almost nothing about horses and, until one spring day in Englishtown, New Jersey, had shown very little interest.

That year we had a good-looking, aggressively social two-year-old colt, aptly named Bad Joke, in the barn, and for some reason my brother took an immediate shine to him. Spencer liked the fact that the dark bay Standardbred colt was interactive and busy-minded and compared him to a great big dog (his words, not mine). Since my brother was doing a whole lot of nothing at the time he decided to stay and work for me for a few months, just so he could learn to take care of the boisterous young horse himself.

The colt was a big jokester. Spencer and he developed a wide range of silly horse-human games that they played, the rules of which were known only to the two of them. My ignorant and unskilled brother taught the colt to fetch, open his stall gate, and stand in his own feed tub, along with all manner of other behaviors that were completely useless to a young racehorse. The reason Bad Joke learned anything at all from my brother was that he wanted to participate in these games, and he not only enjoyed but even reveled in their constant interactions.

To many people, Bad Joke would have been an annoying clown of a horse, one that needed to be kept busy and tired in order to keep him from tearing his stall apart each day out of boredom. To

Spencer, on the other hand, he seemed like a huge friendly puppy, both responsive and fun.

This young horse's personality, however, was responsible for at least some of his training problems. Bad Joke wanted to go out on the racetrack just to socialize. He wasn't at all interested in getting tired every day. Like all young racehorses he needed experience working in a group, so a few times a week he would be included in training "sets" (groups of horses at about the same stage of training). In these situations, he just clowned around, trying to bite and play with the other youngsters, paying no attention to whoever was trying to pilot him at the time. He had little interest in allowing his chubby little body to be molded into a sleek, swift racing machine and consequently made slow to mediocre progress as a potential racehorse. (Not unlike my brother's own personality at that time.) Bad Joke was a bit of a Tom Sawyer type, so it really isn't surprising how well they got on.

I would rate Bad Joke as a 7 or 8 on the aggressivity scale.

PASSIVE   AGGRESSIVE

1	2	3	4	5	6	7	8	9	10

aggressively social

EXAMPLE: *Freesia (passively social)*

A good example of a passively social horse was a three-year-old red bay Arabian filly. Freesia was best described by the word "sweet" because that is what she was. All of the time. She was interested in everything but in a quiet way, content to view her surroundings peacefully and benevolently. Everything I wanted from her she gave me.

It was impossible not to become attached to this filly. She didn't like to cause trouble or be in trouble. Even though she was not the most talented horse I had in training at that time, she was everyone's favorite because of her disposition. If someone made a dumb mistake like leaving the gate open she would stand there patiently, waiting for them to realize she was loose instead of taking advantage of the situation and running down the road or tearing up the yard. Freesia was so content and peaceful that she probably would have let you dress her up in doll clothes and push her around in a stroller if you could have found one that fit. She was that much of a pet.

I would classify her as a social type who was about a 2 on the aggressivity scale.

PASSIVE									AGGRESSIVE
1	2	3	4	5	6	7	8	9	10

▲
passively social

FEARFUL RANGE: Timid to Terrified

A fearful horse sees a world full of potential dangers that must be escaped from, and he needs to be reassured continuously in order to curb his flight instincts. (Do keep your wits about you as you handle this type, because sudden or panicky behavior is harder to manage than a social horse's more deliberate actions.)

What are the differences between a passively fearful horse and an aggressively fearful one? Somewhat shy and watchful but easily reassured, a passively fearful horse bonds with his few chosen people and gains confidence in their presence. A passively fearful horse, well handled and confident, can appear almost social until his confidence is shaken or rocked. The best type of handler or rider for this type is one without fear issues of her own: quiet, low-key, and patient.

An aggressively fearful horse is potentially much more dangerous, because he is more prone to panic than to worry. When this type of horse panics, he becomes very reflexive or reactive, with hair-trigger responses to minimal stimuli. You must be able to see things through the eyes of an aggressively fearful horse in order to handle one correctly, and this skill alone takes years of experience.

As a rule this type is much better off being handled by a confident, skilled, patient, and empathetic horseman. When I rode young Thoroughbreds in Colt's Neck, New Jersey, I had a number of occasions where I was aboard aggressively fearful horses. When they got scared they were prone to bolting (running off at high speed, seemingly blind and oblivious to their surroundings). This can be very unsettling and dangerous for the rider because the horse has withdrawn from the aids and is therefore out of control. I was lucky that neither I nor any of the witless horses I rode under these circumstances was hurt.

Aggressivity can intensify fearful traits in these ways:

▶ **Interaction.** More passive types will be less cautious than their aggressively fearful counterparts.

▶ **Need for personal space.** More aggressively fearful types will be much more claustrophobic than the passive ones.

▶ **Relationship to herd.** More aggressively fearful types need social structure; their comfort level is based on it.

▶ **Adaptability.** The more aggressive they are about their fearful tendencies the longer they take to be comfortable in new locations.

▶ **Reactiveness.** Passively fearful horses are less overreactive than more aggressive ones.

▶ **Flight or fight?** Passive horses will tolerate a little more of a stimulus before choosing the flight option.

▶ **Attention span.** The more passively fearful horse will usually have the longest attention span earlier on.

▶ **Response to training.** The entire range of fearful horses tries hard to comply.

▶ **Lessons and routine.** The entire range prefers a predictable routine.

ALOOF RANGE: Indifferent to Withdrawn

The passively aloof horse may be so quiet as to appear to have no personality at all! His worst crime might be that he may not respond quickly enough to the aids, or signals. He may seem dull or unresponsive to interactions on the ground or under saddle and is best handled by someone who can resist the urge to nag him. Nagging will make a passively aloof horse tune you out even more.

An aggressively aloof horse may studiously ignore not only specific aids but everything else as well. He may appear difficult to connect with and be slow or very sporadic about responding to stimuli. When he finally pays attention to his rider or handler, he

STALLIONS & PERSONALITY

A male horse's personality will not change signifi-cantly after he is gelded. A realistic expectation is that he will slide a few notches toward being more passive in expressing whatever personality type he already has. Nor will gelding fix training problems. All gelding does is take the hormones out of the equation. This alone does have a tendency to make most types easier to handle. For some horses just a move downward on the aggressivity scale can make them suitable for someone who may not have been able to handle them had they remained entire.

After training and working with over eighty stallions in my lifetime, however, I have concluded that they, like the many mares and geldings I have worked with over the years, are products of their personality, their training, and their conformation issues, and nothing more. We had fourteen stallions that performed regularly at the Arabian Nights Dinner Theater in Orlando, and even now we keep between ten and fifteen stallions of various breeds and training levels in our barn at any given time. The stallions themselves are not necessarily a problem. Inept or poor handling of any horse, along with misunderstandings about basic personality issues, will lead to far more complicated problems than simply having a stallion in your program.

may suddenly overreact to an aid sequence that he had previously ignored several times. He may also have a hard time following more complex aid sequences. This type will have the best chance for a successful career if ridden by a quiet rider with firm resolve and very clear aids that remain consistent over time.

Here are some ways aggressivity affects the aloof personality:

▶ **Interaction.** Although most aloof horses are not particularly interactive in herd situations, more passive ones may show more interest in the herd than the aggressively aloof ones.

▶ **Need for personal space.** More passively aloof types may show interest in their people especially once a relationship has been established.

▶ **Relationship to herd.** The more aggressive they are the more independent or removed they will appear.

▶ **Response to aids.** More aggressively aloof horses may appear to studiously ignore the aids, while more passive ones tolerate them.

▶ **Reactiveness.** Aggressively aloof horses may underreact and then suddenly overreact when they finally "tune in."

I received an aggressively aloof Swedish horse for training a few years ago. Although he was not at all fearful, he would spook (come completely off the aids) violently, randomly, and unpredictably. During a short assessment period, I realized that this was just his way of tuning into, or out of, the many training situations or aid sequences that required his attentiveness.

Although he was not at all fearful, he would spook

unpredictably. I quickly realized that this was just his way of

tuning into, or out of, training situations or aid sequences

that required his attentiveness.

For him, spooking was a way to change the channel on whatever I wanted him to do. Each time he spooked, he would erase whatever we were working on and I would have to start again. The horse was a talented dressage mover, agile and athletic, but he needed a training program that incorporated his personality issues along with his training and riding problems. This was the three-step approach I took:

1) I started with a firm understanding that no aid or request should last more than a second.

2) He must respond promptly or the dosage of rein or leg pressure would be increased until I got an answer.

3) As soon as he did answer I would remove the aid and return to "neutral" as a rider — meaning quiet, relaxed, and passive — until he needed further instruction.

Note: This aid sequence might be far different from the small reassuring movements (half halts or leg pressures) I would use on a fearful horse who tensed up, an example of how different types need different stimuli in order to be relaxed and/or productive.

Once we devised a program that suited my intended purpose and the aggressively aloof personality of this Swedish Warmblood horse, his scores at Fourth Level dressage rose into the 70s (a high score for horses at any level, much less Fourth), earning him the United States Dressage Federation (USDF) national ranking of second in the country for that year.

CHALLENGING RANGE: Testing to Threatening

The difference between a passively challenging horse and an aggressively challenging one is the variation, in my opinion, that needs the most attention. A passively challenging horse may not be the most compliant individual and may appear a little testy or opinionated at times. In contrast, an aggressively challenging horse can be quite dangerous, exploiting any weakness he can find in his handling or training program and taking advantage of it.

A passively challenging horse well handled by a clear, firm, and confident rider will resemble a social horse that has good boundaries. These horses make wonderfully brave and confident partners.

Aggressively challenging types enjoy intimidating other horses and even people when they can get away with it. An aggressively challenging horse needs to be carefully handled from birth on so that he becomes aware of his proper place in the horse-human equation. More on handling challenging types in chapter 11.

Aggressivity "colors" the challenging personality as follows:

▶ **Sense of self.** Aggressively challenging horses seem more prideful or arrogant than their passive counterparts.

Kim Barteau and the aggressively challenging stallion Marcel. This horse thrived when performing "at liberty." His story begins on page 83.

▶ **Need for personal space.** Aggressively challenging stallions are among the most guarded and territorial.

▶ **Relationship to herd/humans.** Aggressively challenging mares and stallions will be near the top of the pecking order. Those higher on the scale need constant clarification of their place in the horse-trainer relationship; the more passive, less so.

▶ **Threatening behavior** (such as biting, kicking, charging, or rushing). Exhibited both by aggressive types and by passive ones who have become spoiled or handled without proper clarity and firmness. This type needs to be taught early not to invade their handler's personal space.

▶ **Adaptability.** More aggressive types can be much more defiant than passive ones when resisting new suggestions.

▶ **Reactiveness.** The higher they are on the aggressivity scale the more explosive the reaction can be to a new stimulus.

▶ **Response to aids.** Passive types are mildly confrontational; aggressive types are much more so.

▶ **Fight or flight?** The more aggressive horse is more prone to fight than the passive one.

▶ **Response to training.** All can make reliable, confident partners when properly trained. Aggressively challenging types can be very charismatic and eye-catching.

▶ **Happiest and most content** when "having things their way." Universally true of this type.

Herd Socializing

Some breeders have success turning aggressively challenging young stallions out with their pregnant broodmares, especially when the mares have a strong character themselves, so the mares will socialize the youngster and help define his station in life. The breeders understand the risks involved and the potential for injury to both the mares and the young stallions. After weighing the possible outcomes, they still choose to have their youngsters socialized and reprimanded in a herd-type situation.

Such herd socializing will not help the same horse in his horse-human relationships, unless his human handlers follow the same hierarchy rules that work so well in a herd situation. This personality type needs to be handled fairly and effectively from birth on because these horses are so prone to testing their limits and boundaries. Once an aggressively challenging horse is spoiled (meaning allowed to indulge in misbehaviors or temper tantrums) he can become quite opportunistic and potentially dangerous.

Handle with Care

An aggressively challenging horse is likely to test your authority repeatedly, and your success or failure in handling these altercations fairly and effectively will directly reflect how safe or reliable this horse will be in the future. Even a well-trained horse with a moderately challenging personality may turn into a difficult or dangerous partner if he is sold into less experienced or less knowledgeable hands. I have known well-trained passively challenging types who caused little to no trouble in their previous location become very unruly when they changed owners or trainers and started to test their new environment (as this type is prone to do). When disciplined and handled fairly but firmly these types will regain their true nature.

In short, any horse can behave badly, the way toddlers might try to achieve something by throwing a fit. A clear thought process, an eye toward the desired results, and an understanding of each horse's temperament and training background will afford you the greatest chance for success.

Ride in Your Range

If I were advising someone who wanted to purchase a horse, I would recommend that a timid or inexperienced rider completely avoid both the aggressively fearful and the aggressively challenging horse. Furthermore, such riders should be cautious undertaking an aggressively aloof or aggressively social horse unless they have a good instructor or trainer that they can count on. In short, a more passive personality usually indicates a horse that is easier to handle, ride, and train than its aggressive counterparts.

In short, a more passive personality

usually indicates a horse that is easier to handle, ride,

and train than its aggressive counterparts.

If you are a skilled rider or trainer, on the other hand, you can enjoy much success with the aggressive personality types. When trained and handled properly they sometimes have that extra edge, work ethic, or bit of charisma that can set them apart or make them the winner in a competitive situation.

It is important to note (now and throughout the course of this book) that horses, like people, do not change their basic personality. We can only hope to influence their behavior by first understanding it.

Contributing Influences

As you study horses to determine their type, and the degree to which they express that type, you may wonder why individuals differ so much in their level of intensity. The following factors will affect the passivity or aggressivity of a horse.

Training and Environment

An individual horse may move as many as three or four notches up or down the aggressiveness scale due to environmental or training influences. For example, an aggressively fearful young horse that initially ranked as an 8 or 9 on the scale may mellow down to a 5 or 6 after a year of training and exposure to a quiet, confidence-building environment. A passively challenging gelding, on the other hand, could find himself in the hands of a timid and inexperienced rider, and, because this type is opportunistic, could exploit the situation, grow even more difficult to handle, and move up into the moderately challenging range. Thankfully, though, that same challenging horse will progress back down the aggressivity scale once he gets back into a proper training system.

How a horse behaves on his own time — whether in his stall or in a field, whether alone or with other horses — will give you clues as to which behaviors are his true type and which are the product of either good or bad training and handling. If you cannot match or improve on a horse's current training environment, your horse's personality will be more likely to assert itself, especially if he is more aggressive about expressing his characteristics.

Intelligence and Energy Level

Two final influences on how your horse behaves, learns, and reacts to you are his basic intelligence and the amount of energy he puts into his daily activities. In my experience defining and dealing with the different personality types among equines, these two factors help explain why two horses of the same type may react differently to the same set of circumstances.

My husband, Kim, and I define intelligence in a horse as the ability to both focus on and make use of the information and/or stimuli he receives. Putting it differently, equine intelligence is revealed by how many repetitions a maneuver requires before the horse retains it. Energy level is the amount of effort a horse is naturally willing to commit to any given task.

Horses receive new information all of the time. How they process it depends on their previous experiences, their basic personality type, and their intelligence level. How they respond to it depends on their previous experiences, their basic personality type, and their energy level.

Intelligence and energy level can affect how two horses of similar type may progress in a training situation. A horse that is clever will learn things faster and retain them better. A horse of lower intelligence may take longer to grasp new concepts and may have a harder time retaining new information. A horse who is unwilling to commit very much energy toward his behavior is usually a more passive type regardless of whether he is social, fearful, aloof, or challenging.

PART TWO

THE FOUR HORSE PERSONALITY TYPES

A detailed look at each

of the four horse personality types

with individual case studies

*In a riding situation,
there are many considerations beyond
which horse you look the best on and how
quickly you might progress. Riding is about
relationships, and all relationships take
effort and understanding if they are going
to survive and thrive. Both parties in any
relationship should be aware of their own
and their partner's strengths and
weaknesses so that they can meet
somewhere in the middle.*

CHAPTER THREE

THE SOCIAL HORSE

THE SOCIAL HORSE IS AN INTERACTIVE CREATURE. Of the four personality types, he is the most interested in the world around him, whether passively, moderately, or aggressively. If someone were to describe a horse as a pet with petlike personality traits, it would almost certainly be a social horse.

The official greeters in the equine world, social horses show more interest in their human's arrival (with or without food) than does any other type. They seek out petting and social interactions more than the other three types do. They tend to be more forgiving, startle less easily, and adapt to new environments more quickly than their fearful, aloof, and challenging counterparts do.

On the other hand, social horses suffer more from distractibility than the other personalities do. The more aggressively social they are, the more easily distracted they can be, especially among youngsters. They also prefer socializing with other horses and may expect you to play second fiddle to their turnout or "friend time."

Although they excel in many disciplines, from racing to Western pleasure, they are especially suited for trick-training and dressage. Both of these occupations depend on a horse's close and consistent communication with his handler or rider, something with which the social horse is naturally comfortable.

CASE STUDY: *Little Chief*

PASSIVE   AGGRESSIVE

| 1 | 2 | 3 | 4 | 5 | 6 | 7 | 8 | 9 | 10 |

▲
moderately social

The first real flesh-and-blood horse I ever met, at age ten, I would now define as a social type. I will guess that Little Chief was somewhere in the lower-middle (more passive) section of the aggressivity scale. He was an Appaloosa, dark with a blanket of spots over his hindquarters, and he probably stood about 15 hands high. I remember his friendly personality more than I remember his looks. But what made the biggest impression on me, an awestruck kid who had only read about horses or seen them on television, was that he was real, and he seemed to want to meet me.

A small herd of tired, dusty trail horses was enjoying a day off, grazing on the sparse grass that grew in the field across the Humber River near where I lived. I had been told many times to stay away from that river, but I had never been told that if horses suddenly appeared on the other side I shouldn't cross over to see them. So I did. While all of the other horses either ignored me or scowled at me, as I now realize tired, overworked trail horses are prone to do, the friendly young Appaloosa did not. He made his way directly toward me with his ears up and an interested, almost welcoming, look on his face.

The minute I laid eyes on him I named him Little Chief, and we hit it off immediately. We took turns following each other around. I petted him, scratched him, picked grass for him to eat (which he seemed to prefer over picking it himself), and spent much of that first visit just staring at him and grinning from ear to ear. I'm sure a rocket ship could have landed beside us on the field and I wouldn't have noticed.

I was finally interrupted, but much too soon, by the trail guide and a few helpers coming to bring in the herd. A bossy, incredibly lucky girl (lucky because she had access to real live horses regularly), sitting astride a bareback horse, warned me to stay away from all of the horses, especially the young Appaloosa. He wasn't even broke yet and I could be hurt, I was informed.

Even at the ignorant age of ten, I knew instinctively that regardless of the amount of training he may or may not have had, the friendly young horse was unlikely to hurt me. He just wanted to socialize and I was a possible companion. I left that day, but returned many times to visit my spotted, social friend. That, however, is another story.

CONCLUSIONS

How did I identify Little Chief as a social horse when I was just a kid? By paying very close attention to him and being interested enough to watch and remember his actions. In particular, I observed a couple of concrete personality clues as I watched and interacted with him.

1) He was interested in me, a stranger, even while on his own time, turned out with other horses, and not really contained (an important defining characteristic of most social horses).

2) He tolerated and welcomed me (someone he was unfamiliar with) into his personal space, even though he was a relatively unhandled youngster.

CASE STUDY: *Redson*

| 1 | 2 | 3 | 4 | 5 | 6 | 7 | 8 | 9 | 10 |

▲

moderately to aggressively social

My husband, Kim, and I had been at Indian Hills training center in Gilberts, Illinois, for less than six months when we met Redson, a bright red bay with little white. His sire, Liberty, an imported Dutch Warmblood, had a passively social personality, while his dam, Ruth, an unraced Thoroughbred, had a mixture of challenging and aloof characteristics.

Redson was born out in a fifty-acre pasture, so we didn't see him until several hours after his birth. His mother was not welcoming when we approached to check out her new foal. She pinned her ears back angrily and inserted herself between the foal and us, showing us her hind legs and unshod hooves in the process.

- -

Redson showed up every day to work with ears up and

an interested, interactive look on his face.

- -

The little colt would have none of it. Despite his mother's angry attempts to run interference, he was interested in us right away. No matter how hard she tried to keep him away, he would wander around or behind her and approach us head on, again and again. He was friendly and charming, at ease with us immediately, and he seemed content to let us fuss over him even as Ruth stomped and scowled insults and threats at us. We kept the visit short, made some mental notes, and then allowed the mare to herd her little charmer away.

Ruth had very little effect on Redson's obviously social personality. He constantly wandered away from her to browse among the herd, make friends, socialize, and visit with any stranger that stopped by. Ruth could not convince him it would be much better first to get angry and then to ignore whoever crossed their paths. Redson, bless his heart, remained true to his innate character.

As a social youngster, he was understandably dismayed to find himself alone in a stall at weaning time, but he did not panic and soon settled in to inspect his new surroundings. He spent about a week in the barn, where he welcomed all of the attention he received and watched with interest as people and horses passed by his stall. He quickly discovered that if he turned his head just right he could fit it between the bars on his door and stick his little nose out there to be petted whenever anyone approached his domain. When he was turned out with the other weanlings, he buddied up with another aggressively social colt, and they took to jumping back and forth between the paddocks just to satisfy their expanding curiosities.

Redson was gelded as a yearling and started under saddle late in his second year. The starting process went smoothly and without incident, and he seemed happy to participate in the "training game." After a few weeks of riding, we turned him back out for the winter and resumed with him the next spring. He was delighted to be part of the program again and showed up every day to work with ears up and an interested, interactive look on his face.

Now five, Redson belongs to a client of ours who was looking for something more than gaits and talent in her next dressage horse. She wanted a horse that would bond and interact with her, one that would happily make the journey up the levels as her partner. The match was perfect. Even though Redson loves his feed, he will leave his bucket of grain to greet Diane whenever she appears.

If he turned his head just right he could stick

his nose out to be petted whenever anyone approached.

CONCLUSIONS

Redson defined himself as a social horse the day he was born, and as he grew his personality remained consistent. Here are four clues:

1) He was eager to interact with us and with other horses.

2) He was less worried and panicky at weaning time than most other babies (a typical social trait).

3) He was interactive and calm about the entire training process.

4) He would leave his own feed bucket to socialize, another trait that many social horses share.

I classified him as a moderately aggressive social horse. This would put him at about a 7 out of 10 on the aggressivity scale before he was gelded, and about a 5 or 6 after that.

CASE STUDY: *HAS Haleys Comet*

PASSIVE   AGGRESSIVE

1	2	3	4	5	6	7	8	9	10

moderately to aggressively social

A clearly social Arabian stallion, Comet falls in the low middle of the aggressivity scale. He has no definable characteristics of any other personality type.

I met Comet early in his third year, while I was working at the Arabian Nights Dinner Theater in Orlando, Florida. Comet had never been off the farm where he was born until he moved from Lexington, Kentucky, to Arabian Nights that spring. His owners, friends of ours, wanted us to start the youngster and, if things worked out, to use him as a featured horse in one of the acts. They sent us some photographs. He was a beautiful and personable-looking liver chestnut stallion, so we agreed to give him a try.

When he arrived from his long trip, I told Jerry, his owner and transporter, to turn him loose in the indoor arena, so he could stretch his legs a little bit before we settled him into a stall. I followed them out past the main curtain into the arena so I could get a good look at him. Even though he had never been away from his small, quiet farm he seemed immediately at home in his new environment.

The indoor auditorium at Arabian Nights should have been quite imposing for a little homebred like Comet, but he looked as comfortable trotting around the arena as the horses that had lived and worked in the show for years. The seating area allows twelve hundred people to eat dinner while they watch the show, and the

SOCIAL
PERSONALITY CHARACTERISTICS

▶ *Interaction.* Interested in observing and interacting with their environment.

▶ *Need for personal space.* Tolerant of people or other horses in their personal space. Appear almost welcoming.

▶ *Relationship to herd.* Rarely at the top of the pecking order but often second or friend to the chief.

▶ *Vocalizing.* Often more vocal than other personality types.

▶ *Adaptability.* Generally accepting of new experiences.

▶ *Weaning.* More confident, less worried and panicky at weaning time than most other foals.

▶ *Reactiveness.* Generally tend to underreact to a new stimulus; not usually explosive.

▶ *Attention span.* Attention span can be very short, especially in youngsters. May have trouble focusing on one thing in a busy environment. May leave own feed bucket to socialize.

▶ *Response to training.* Once trained are usually steady performers; will need occasional tune-ups on basic issues.

▶ *Lessons & routine.* Appreciate variety in their lessons.

▶ *Tolerance of poor handling.* Tend to be more tolerant of inept or poor handling than other types.

▶ *Happiest & most content* when allowed to interact with other horses, people, and the environment.

▶ *Breeds that may be associated with a social-type personality:* Friesians, many draft breeds, Arabians, Morgans, many warmbloods, many Andalusians.

Beth Noteman and HAS Haleys Comet at Lamplight
Show Grounds, Wayne, Illinois.

arena has a large stage overhead at one end and a skybox up high at the other. Underneath the skybox was the potentially very scary area we referred to as the Black Hole.

The Black Hole was a curtained-off storage area containing props and cables for some of the acts. Inside was a small holding stall where we would tie the unicorn (a live horse that would masquerade as a unicorn and who performed a hind leg walk from one end of the arena to the other) before the audience arrived each evening. A fog machine and the opening jumps were against the inside wall. It always smelled a little musty in there, and we often left the curtain open during the day to let it air out a little.

Many of the horses that worked in the show every day were afraid of the Black Hole and would spook, snort, and stare every time they passed by. Comet was not in the least intimidated. After circling the arena in an investigatory sort of manner, he lowered his neck, trotted up to the Black Hole, and walked right in!

I dashed across the arena, thinking he would frighten himself and get tangled in the props back there, but I needn't have worried. When I reached the entrance I observed Comet calmly nosing around among all of the props in a most unconcerned fashion.

I turned to his owner and said, "Oh yes, he can stay. In fact, if you have any more at home just like him, you should go get them right now."

Comet was not in the least intimidated.

After circling the arena in an investigatory sort of manner,

he lowered his neck, trotted up to the Black Hole,

and walked right in!

Comet was a breeze to start. Unfortunately he never did perform in the dinner show because our whole family moved about eight months later. His owners wanted him to stay in our training program and they asked us to bring him up to Illinois and find a buyer for him. So we did.

Shortly after settling up north I received a call from a sales executive named Beth Noteman. Her beloved gray Arabian mare had recently passed away, and she heard I had a gray Arabian mare in training. Could she come see her? After chatting briefly about her level of riding experience and the expectations she would have of her new mount, we agreed on a date for her to come and see the gray mare and a few others I had for sale.

I liked Beth as soon as I met her. She is the kind of person who makes a very good first impression. Respectful of our time, she still wanted the benefit of our expertise and was very attentive as I described the three horses I had picked for her to try out. She only interrupted me once.

When I mentioned the young liver chestnut stallion, now four years old, she raised a hand and said politely, "I am an amateur rider just starting in dressage. I'm not sure a stallion would be appropriate for me."

"Well, you can always geld him," I replied. "He really is special. Why don't you just give him a look?"

Politely, she agreed to look at all of the horses. The gray mare first, then a bay gelding with a little more training and some show experience on him, and finally Comet.

To make a long story short, after riding the three horses that day and the next, she ended up buying Comet. This savvy stranger took a leap of faith and listened to a horse trainer she had just met tell her which horse she would be the most compatible with. Six years later he is still a stallion and she is still an amateur rider, but they are working on the Prix St. Georges and he is the love of her life. She dotes on him, and he thrives on it. They are great friends and show partners, and together they have won more awards and National Championships than any other purebred Arabian dressage stallion and amateur rider in the fifty-year history of Arabian show horses.

Six years later he is still a stallion and she is still an amateur rider, but they are working on the Prix St. Georges and he is the love of her life. She dotes on him, and he thrives on it.

CONCLUSIONS

Comet defined himself to me as a social horse within minutes of my meeting him. Here were four signs:

1) He left the farm he was born on for the first time, went on a long trailer ride, and settled himself into a new environment with little to no anxiety and clear interest in his new surroundings — a definite social trait.

2) Very self-confident, Comet was not afraid of the Black Hole, as most horses were to some degree or another.

3) He was easy to start under saddle.

4) While he has remained a stallion, he is still trustworthy to handle and ride, even by an amateur.

Using these clues, I assigned Comet a 5 on the aggressivity scale.

CASE STUDY: *Beau Pres*

PASSIVE   AGGRESSIVE

1	2	3	4	5	6	7	8	9	10

aggressively social

One of the horses at the Arabian Nights Dinner Theater in Orlando was a comical eleven-year-old fleabitten gray Arabian gelding named Beau Pres. A bit player in the show, he participated in the drills but never rose to the status of high school or solo horse.

Beau Pres was an aggressively social jokester. He had mastered a variety of snaps and knots and enjoyed untying the other horses as they stood on the wall next to him waiting for drill practice. No one, be he man or horse, could get by him without getting whacked by his tail. His aim was remarkable.

It was his natural interest in interacting with things behind him that inspired us to select and train him as one of the beach-ball-kicking horses for the show. He quickly learned to kick the balls as they were thrown to him, and his aim was so good he could send them flying right out of the arena. Because he enjoyed his beachball training, he hit the ball more accurately and reliably than the other two horses that were trained for that act.

Unfortunately for Beau Pres, he was not an attractive horse. Taller than the other Arabians, lanky, and a bit homely headed, he just didn't look as appealing as the two bouncier, prettier horses wearing the costume that was an important part of the "Florida Horse" act. Consequently, he had to be content with second and third string for that particular routine. Lynn (one of the assistant trainers and his favorite person at the barn) would often take him out in the arena and let him kick the balls around, just for fun.

A busybody who just could not keep to himself, Beau Pres found ways to interact with the other horses at the show, whether they were working in the arena with him or passing by in the barn aisle. He was aggressively friendly, with a repertoire of facial expressions that he used to communicate with and to get attention. He was also the classic bucket banger, having learned that if he made enough of a racket somebody would come and visit him (even if it was just to reprimand him and take his bucket away).

He was also the horse we used most frequently for the riding auditions at the show. Although he would not try his hardest unless you were fairly skilled, his amiable, friendly demeanor helped to reduce some of the anxieties of the hopeful candidates.

CONCLUSIONS

Beau Pres was almost eleven years old when I first met him, which leads me to believe he was probably quite a fun handful as a youngster. He was clearly aggressively social, and here were three clues:

1) Beau Pres was very interactive with both horses and humans.

2) A colorful character, he wanted interaction so badly that he devised all manner of attention-getting behaviors.

3) He was able to observe his surroundings while still remaining at ease in a variety of situations. This is the best and most observable characteristic of most social horses.

Because of the extent of his interest in interaction, I would label him around an 8 on the passive-aggressive scale. If he had remained a stallion, he probably would have been a 10.

CHAPTER FOUR

THE FEARFUL HORSE

THANKS TO MANY OF THE BOOKS I READ AS A CHILD, I assumed (before I met any actual equines) that most horses would have fearful-type personalities. Many new riders make the same assumption and thus treat every horse as a fearful type until they learn more. I have found fearful horses to be more common among certain breeds but not in the overall horse population. By nature horses are often sensitive, alert, and quick to respond, but that does not mean they are fearful.

Having a preconceived notion about horses may block our ability to see each individual clearly. Always wait for the horse himself, or a trusted advisor, to give you the information necessary to identify any given type. That being said, fearful types, especially the passive ones, tend to mellow out a bit with age, careful handling, and proper training. Thus they are easiest to spot when they are youngsters or early in their training days.

Ranging from quietly watchful and shy to claustrophobic and panicky, fearful horses are easily startled and defensive. They like people as much as social horses do and tend to bond even more strongly with trusted individuals. Unlike some of the other personality types, fearful horses usually pay close attention to circumstances, and they are therefore less likely to tolerate or ignore unfair or rough treatment than an aloof or social horse.

Although they are interested in their environment, fearful horses are not always comfortable with change. They need reassurance and time to gain confidence in almost anything new. New procedures, environments, and even handlers need to be introduced quietly and carefully.

Many fearful horses get a little too attached or dependent on their equine buddies and may have strong reactions (which may be misinterpreted as misbehavior) when they are separated. Horses of this personality type may injure themselves more frequently at weaning time because their insecurity and panic is greater than that of other types, especially when young.

CASE STUDY: *Jetinski*

PASSIVE | | | | | | | | | AGGRESSIVE

| 1 | 2 | 3 | 4 | 5 | 6 | 7 | 8 | 9 | 10 |

passively to moderately fearful

When I was eighteen, shortly after I had started to work as a groom for a Standardbred racing stable at Greenwood Racetrack in Ontario, Canada, I was assigned to care for a coming three-year-old trotter named Jetinski. This big bay filly with a fearful personality had yet to achieve any success as a racehorse, mostly because her nervousness escalated rapidly into a state of near-panic whenever she was hooked to a jog cart or a race bike and headed toward the track.

Most racehorses start their career when they are young, and many young, fearful horses need someone to bond with in order to be comfortable in the busy and often overwhelming racetrack environment. The horses that don't seem to settle in become a subject of some concern to their trainers. It was not uncommon for some of the old racetrackers to put a young goat in the stall with a fearful type, hoping the horse would bond a little bit with the smaller animal, settle down some, eat its feed, and just relax. We didn't have any goats at our stable, since the trainer that I worked for did not subscribe to the goat theory at the time. When I met Jetinski she was a lost and worried filly who had not yet found peace in her environment.

The backstretch of any racetrack can be a very busy place, and Greenwood Racetrack was no exception. With more than sixty horses in training at our stable and more than two hundred total on the backstretch, a young, fearful horse could easily become overwhelmed. While Jetinski had shown some talent for trotting at speed, she had been unreliable about maintaining her trot under pressure (which was constant) or in the company of other horses.

In addition, she was underweight and wouldn't finish her meals, and there were several reasons for this. First, the stable had rules about feeding. All horses were fed at the same time, and forty-five minutes after feed time the tubs were pulled from the stall and cleaned for the next feeding. Jetinski had usually eaten only a few handfuls by the time her bucket was pulled. Second, she stall-walked while she was eating, grabbing a bite and then pacing nervously around the stall with the feed dribbling out of her mouth.

I embarked on a project with the nervous filly, after requesting permission from John, the head trainer, to alter her routine. When feed time came, I brought in her feed and then stayed with her while she ate. I restrained her from walking around and stood by her, talking and petting her neck until she finished her ration.

FEARFUL
PERSONALITY CHARACTERISTICS

▶ *Interaction.* Guarded or cautious (especially as youngsters).

▶ *Need for personal space.* May indicate a need for more personal space than they have; may be somewhat claustrophobic when uncomfortable or confined.

▶ *Vocalizing.* Usually vocalize out of anxiety or loneliness, and upon the arrival, with or without food, of someone they have bonded with.

▶ *Adaptability.* Not immediately at ease in new situations.

▶ *Reactiveness.* May have strong, quick, or reflexive-type reactions to stimuli or aids. Could be described as over-reactive.

▶ *Fight or flight?* More flight- than fight-oriented.

▶ *Relationship to herd.* Very dependent on social structure. Likely to bond with another horse or human.

▶ *Behavior quirks.* May be poor eaters; may be stall walkers.

▶ *Weaning.* May be insecure and panicky at weaning time.

▶ *Attention span.* Once comfortable, often have a long attention span.

▶ *Response to training.* Once trained, usually make very strong efforts to comply. Not tolerant of poor treatment.

▶ *Lessons & routine.* Prefer consistent, predictable routines; have trouble adjusting to multiple riders.

▶ *Happiest & most content* when in the reassuring presence of a stronger personality, either human or equine.

▶ *Breeds that may be associated with a fearful-type personality:* Thoroughbreds, Arabians, some warmbloods.

I also cut her grain in half so she had a better chance to complete her meal in a short time. I did this for all of her meals, gradually increasing the amount of grain she was receiving until she was back to her required amount. She liked having me with her, and I soon took to grooming her while she ate.

There were other problems, however, outside her stall. She was afraid of the racetrack and its busy atmosphere, so I took her for long walks in-hand in the afternoon when it was quieter and the horses were through training for the day. At first she wouldn't relax and was hard to handle, but after about a week she became much easier to manage.

Quickly, the filly's attachment to me became obvious. She watched me as I worked with my other two horses and whinnied every time I entered the barn aisle. She would not stand still for the blacksmith unless I was holding her.

Soon all that remained to be addressed was her erratic behavior during her jog and training miles. Normally, it took three people to hook her to her jog cart each morning. I was assigned to hold her while another groom and one of the trainers attached the shafts of the cart to her harness. She would prance in place during this process, and as soon as I let her go and John climbed into the cart, she would go skidding and scrambling off as if her tail was on fire.

Once on the track she was even worse. Head up, eyes wild and bulging, she leaned on the reins and raced around as if trying to outrun the very cart she was hitched to. I arranged to jog the filly myself, in the afternoon when the track was quieter, to try to calm her down and help her gain confidence, and permission was quickly granted.

The challenge would be hooking her up by myself. Almost all work in a racing stable happens before noon, and no one would be around to bail me out if she got away from me during the afternoon hours. I proceeded slowly and cautiously the first day, hooking a lead line to the cavesson of her bridle and keeping a hand on it at all times. Hitching her up took quite a while, but I didn't lose her.

I made her walk up to the track and then walk for a long time once she got up there. It was hard; I had to almost halt her, then walk a few steps, then almost halt again, all the while talking to her in an encouraging voice. When I finally let her trot, she tried to take off. I brought her back to a walk and repeated the process until she would trot without trying to take off. We were out there for an hour and a half that first day, but things soon improved.

Within a week she was jogging around the track on a soft rein, with no tension or carrying on during the hitching process. Her training or "speed" miles became much more productive because she was no longer burning nervous energy in her warmups or walking her stall. During her three-year-old year she won more than $65,000 racing in sires stakes races, and she broke the track record for three-year-old trotting fillies at one of the half-mile tracks in Orangeville, Ontario.

At the end of the racing season, she was sold to become a broodmare for a large breeding operation somewhere in Europe, and I was sad to see her go. She had become beautiful during the course of the year. Her big frame had filled out with the feed and hard work, and her coat glistened with health. She was also quiet and content, a far cry from the nervous underweight filly I had started the season with.

CONCLUSIONS

Jetinski was easy to define as a fearful type, and here's why:

1) She showed nervous-type reactions and behaviors almost constantly when I first met her.

2) She was a stall walker and a poor eater (typical fearful traits).

3) She had a hard time adapting to new or very busy places.

4) She bonded very clearly with me, so much so that my presence was required in order for her to feel comfortable with anything new.

5) She had very quick, defensive, and reactionary responses to unsettling situations.

I would have classified her as a 7 on the aggressivity scale when I met her and about a 3 or 4 by the time she was trained and sold.

CASE STUDY: *Countache*

PASSIVE | AGGRESSIVE

1 2 3 4 5 6 7 8 9 10

moderately fearful

I worked with a bay Arabian gelding named Countache at the Arabian Nights Dinner Theater in Florida. He was athletic and talented and had benefited from some good training at various times during his life, but the training had been sporadic and, consequently, so was he. Flighty and unpredictable, he was on hiatus from the show when I started there because he was too annoying and time-consuming to work with. At seven years old he was well developed, handsome, and talented enough for many of the routines, but he had not finished with the training he needed for the high-school routines (upper-level dressage movements). In addition, he was a little too claustrophobic and sporadic in his responses to the aids to be reliable, even in the easier drills.

Needing a couple of project horses to work with and hopefully improve (as part of my training responsibilities), I chose Countache as one of them. Without time to be his groom (the best way to bond with a horse), I had to take advantage of some small interactions before and after I rode him each day in the hope of gaining his trust.

Countache was busy-minded, thinking about everything at once and nothing at all. He needed to settle down enough to focus and listen to me. I made him walk a long time in those early days while I sat quietly and waited for him to focus on three basics: the connection from hand to mouth, going to the bit, and his walk rhythm. I had no real pressure to make immediate progress with this horse because he wasn't needed in the show at present.

Within a couple of weeks Countache was walking and trotting respectably on the bit. As his focus and concentration became more reliable, I started with some canter and lateral work. To help him concentrate and make him softer in the back I worked him a little overly round and deep early on. That phrase means the poll of the horse is lower than the withers and the nose is behind the vertical so that the back comes up a bit rounder than normal. The horse is still lightly connected to and going toward the bit and should always be ahead of the leg in this work. I use it as an attention-getting or suppling exercise.

*Countache and I performing
at the Arabian Nights Dinner
Theater, Orlando, Florida.*

Within six months he was ready to attempt some of the more difficult dressage acts in the show. He could not, however, become accustomed to a new routine while performing it during the evening show, the way some of the other more confident horses did. He needed rehearsals. Tech and costuming needed to be tried out a minimum of three or four times before he could be counted on to stay calm in front of an audience with any new routine.

Like other fearful horses, Countache did not enjoy having multiple riders, and he performed at his best with either myself or Chrissy, a talented and quiet rider who suited him well. In order to keep his confidence intact, his afternoon work, his preshow warm-up, and even the person assigned to tack or untack him each day remained as consistent as possible. Overall, Countache was a fine and spirited horse, moderately fearful, who needed some special attention, to which he responded well.

CONCLUSIONS

Countache was described as flighty and unpredictable when I met him, and these words are often associated with fearful horses. Here's how I recognized his type:

1) He was extremely uncomfortable with sporadic training efforts and responded best to a routine he was comfortable with (a distinct fearful trait).

2) His active mind made it hard for him to settle down to work.

3) He had trouble adapting to multiple riders and handlers, since his hard-gained confidence could be easily compromised in the wrong hands.

I would have classified Countache at about a 6 on the passive-aggressive scale when I met him and about a 3 or 4 after less than a year of training.

COUNTACHE'S DAILY ROUTINE

Like most fearful horses, Countache liked routine. He liked to warm up the same way every day, take a walk break, and then concentrate on his real work for fifteen or twenty minutes. At the end of his ride he enjoyed standing on a long rein and watching the other horses in the ring for a few minutes before going back to his stall.

CHAPTER FIVE

THE ALOOF HORSE

THE ALOOF HORSE IS EASIEST to define by what he doesn't do. Aloof types interact much less than any of the other types do, and at times this horse may seem to be in his own little world. He will frequently seem detached or removed from his present environment, to the point of being disassociated from it. Owners of aloof horses frequently notice this detachment or distance, as if their horse had an invisible barrier around him. It may appear that your aloof horse is paying very close or studious attention to almost nothing at all.

Some horses of this type may be referred to as "numb" or "dull" by their trainers, as if they can't even feel the aids. An astute observer may note a rather glazed or removed look in the aloof horse's eyes, even while trying to interact with them. In fact, an aloof horse seems to avoid interactions with both humans and fellow equines whenever possible. This personality type has a tendency to tolerate the riding aids or to tune them out, rather than respond to them promptly.

Aloof horses will rarely "start" an interaction, but that does not mean that they don't need them. Be sure when you interact with an aloof horse that he does respond. Ignoring interaction is far too easy for this type.

A lovely young Dutch Warmblood mare was already boarding at Indian Hills when we first moved there from Florida. A 16-hand china doll of a horse, Kyra was a light bay with four white feet and a white nose. She had an Arabian-type head, big doe eyes that seemed to have black eyeliner around them, and a dancer's way of handling her compact body. She caught my eye and my interest the first time I saw her, but because she was not part of my training program I paid only peripheral attention to her for the next year or so.

At that point her owner asked me to help her represent and market the beautiful mare, since the two were not making much progress in moving up the dressage levels. I took Kyra in training and soon "pegged" her as a passively aloof horse that would become more aggressively aloof or disassociative under pressure. She did not want to stay involved in her work, and while she never initiated any misbehaviors, she tended to tolerate rather than answer the most basic and vital riding aids. If these aids increased in duration or intensity, Kyra would overreact, jumping and leaping around in a most athletic fashion, and then tune me out again.

I did what any skilled and experienced trainer would do and went back to basics, looking for the holes in her training process and any lack of understanding of the aids. Her training problems were tangled up with her personality issues like a big ball of twine. I oversimplified everything for her, kept my rides short and positive,

Kyra and owner Gail Rodecker at a show in Indiana.

and when she did throw one of her hissy fits, I did not overreact or lose track of the response I needed from her.

Her behavior in the barn was generally quiet and complacent. She was not really interested in the activities in the barn unless she knew that feed time was imminent. When she felt put-upon by an overstimulating ride, she would retreat to the back of the stall and keep her head in the corner until the next feeding. She also did not form any attachments to horses and preferred to be turned out alone.

- -

She was not really interested in the activities

in the barn unless she knew that feed time was imminent.

- -

As I simplified her work for her, giving her intermittent information and additional chances to relax and understand the aids, she became less explosive and more responsive in her daily work. She was eventually sold to another student of mine, a quiet but systematic rider whose only problem was her lack of broad experiences and access to a regular lesson program. Their progress has been slow but steady. Her new owner can now do all of the Third-Level work with her, while I can ride her almost happily through the Prix St. George.

Kyra is an example of a passively aloof-type horse that retreated into more aggressively aloof behavior under saddle because of her training difficulties. The solution: lots of simple basics and time to process her learning.

CONCLUSIONS

It took a while for Kyra to identify herself to me as a passively aloof personality (a 3 or 4 on the aggressivity scale) because she had so many training issues. Here are three clues I detected:

1) She always kept to herself, as far as other horses were concerned. She actually preferred to be turned out alone.

2) She tended to tolerate rather than respond to or interact with her rider or handler. She remained somewhat detached from her new owner, who took care of her every day.

3) She was prone at times to general unresponsiveness, tuning out the aids.

ALOOF

▶ *Interaction.* Not particularly interactive in herd situations.

▶ *Need for personal space.* Tolerate, but don't always welcome, intrusion in their personal space.

▶ *Relationship to herd/humans.* May appear somewhat independent of both horses and people.

▶ *Behavior quirks.* May exhibit disassociative-type behavior, such as cribbing or weaving.

▶ *Response to aids.* Often seem to have a delayed reaction — sometimes strong, sometimes very slight — to stimuli or aids. Reaction time is slower than in other types. Will often appear to deliberately shut out all sources of stimulation, including rider aids.

▶ *Reactiveness.* Generally not prone to explosive behaviors; show natural restraint.

▶ *Response to training.* Once trained will need occasional reality checks.

▶ *Happiest & most content* when allowed ample "alone time."

▶ *Breeds that may be associated with aloof-type personalities:* Lipizzans, Hanoverians, Russian horses in general, Quarter Horses, Trakehners, Akhal Tekes.

CASE STUDY: *Bentley*

PASSIVE   AGGRESSIVE

1	2	3	4	5	6	7	8	9	10

▲

aggressively aloof

Recently I was at a dressage show at Lamplight Equestrian Center in Wayne, Illinois. During any dressage competition there is always talk among the trainers about horses new to the area, and I heard that a Danish Warmblood was for sale. Since there are always horses for sale everywhere, I just kept track of the information until I matched it up with the poorly trained but incredible athlete that I spotted in the warm-up arena.

I followed the rather plainly marked dark bay gelding over to the show ring to watch his Third Level test and he impressed me even more. Lots of training issues on display, definitely some disconnect in the personality department, but a very inspiring and impressive athlete nonetheless. I mentioned the nimble-footed gelding to a friend and colleague who was rather casually looking for a second horse. She was a good rider with FEI skills, and we agreed that I would test-ride him in front of her the next day.

The horse was silly with talent, with three huge gaits and a catlike balance in his movements. Less than thirty minutes into my test ride, the client, myself, and about twenty others standing around the arena could see that this was one heck of a horse. His talent for the FEI movements far outweighed his training troubles, so an offer was made for him that day.

Negotiations were completed, vetting performed, and after some small delays in the delivery, Bentley became our project. We were excited to begin.

Bentley and Kassie Barteau
perform a pirouette at
Lamplight, Illinois.

His training issues were many, mostly basics gone wrong or overlooked altogether. He didn't steer from the leg, had no understanding of the half-halt, and was very stiff in his back, to the point of being unresponsive laterally on both sides. He had also perfected the charming habit of retracting and locking his poll against almost every rein aid. All of these problems, however, while a little time-consuming, were eminently fixable.

The other issue to be considered and then factored into the training equation was his personality. As mentioned, aloof horses are easiest to read because of what they don't do, and Bentley was true to type. He did not appear to be a troublemaker until I refused to pull on the reins; then he refused to acknowledge or respond to the leg aids, and we ended up out of the arena, down the driveway, and out in the middle of the street.

Even when he disassociated from a direct aid, as aloof horses are prone to do, Bentley took matters one step further. Ignoring simple steering requests, he would dash around the arena in a haphazard fashion, zoning out from his own misbehavior and all of my attempts to connect with him using the standard aids (seat, leg, and hand). He wasn't necessarily misbehaving in an outward kind of way; he was just tuning me out, like a kid who puts his hands over his ears and says "la la la" while you are trying to talk to him. During our first training session together I classified him at about an 8 on the aggressivity scale in terms of his aloof personality traits.

He wasn't necessarily misbehaving; he was just tuning

me out, like a kid who puts his hands over his ears and says

"la la la" while you are trying to talk to him.

I was excited about the Bentley project, finding his combination of personality, training issues, and talent an inspiring challenge. The answer to any training problem is always in the basics, and that is where we went. With aloof horses, training issues often become related to personality issues because of this type's tendency to "tune out" important interactions. It is important for the rider to remember that understanding and responding to the proper aids will solve almost all riding problems.

Since this type tends not to pay attention to what is actively happening in front of them, or even to them, they often have a delayed or insufficient response to the aids. This can inspire a rider or trainer to nag with the aids or keep the aids on for too long, causing the aloof horse to tune the requests out even more. Bentley was exactly that way. First I had to apply clear, sharp aids to get Bentley's attention. Once he put an ear toward me to show that he was focused on me, I would apply the appropriate aids for whatever movement I was seeking. Applying the aids properly is always about the right aid, the right timing, and the correct dosage for the situation at hand.

Bentley spent a few rides investigating his options, doing his best to studiously ignore my requests, but I was not to be deterred. Soon enough he caught on to the program and has been responding beautifully since then in a steady and progressive way. He is still an amazing athlete, and now that he is in an environment where he is being trained instead of just being ridden each day, he is making tangible, bordering on rapid, progress. He will start his first season at FEI this year as one of the most talented horses I have ever had the opportunity to work with.

If he had not been so incredibly gifted as a dressage mover, he may have had difficulty in this sport because of the constant small interactions that need to be responded to in order to make progress. Bentley's huge benefit is that, physically, the work is very easy for him, so the only real problem he faces is his attention to the aids. Keeping these requests clear, consistent, and as small as possible affords him the best chance at success.

Most days Bentley gets turned out after work with another gelding, an aggressively aloof and somewhat challenging character named Angelo. I enjoy watching them together. Since they both have aggressively aloof personalities but are still herd animals by nature, they do seem to prefer to be turned out together rather than alone. They orbit rather casually around each other in the big field, each keeping more or less to himself. Even upon closer observation they look exactly like what they are: two aggressively aloof horses who enjoy being alone together.

CONCLUSIONS

Bentley is an aggressively-aloof horse without discernible traits from the other personality types. Even though he is a gelding, he is still about an 8 on the passive-aggressive scale. Had he remained a stallion, he would have undoubtedly been a 10, making him the most aggressively aloof horse I have ever met.

He was easy for me to identify because of the glazed or somewhat "removed" look in his eye, but readers new to defining type may need more tangible clues. Here are four:

1) He seemed disconnected from both his rider and his environment when I first observed him at a show grounds.

2) He paid no attention to anything happening around him.

3) He showed little or no interest in interacting with me on the ground when I first handled him. I could have been anybody or nobody: humans were all the same to him.

4) He was slow and/or sporadic about responding to very obvious rein and leg aids.

CASE STUDY: *Pluto Bertha*

PASSIVE   AGGRESSIVE

| 1 | 2 | 3 | 4 | 5 | 6 | 7 | 8 | 9 | 10 |

aggressively aloof

Among the Lippizan geldings at the Arabian Nights Dinner Theater was an aggressively aloof character named Pluto Bertha. Bertha was a cribber, meaning that he would habitually grasp a solid object (such as a door or ledge) with his teeth and suck in air. This vice appears more often in aloof types than in any other, but that does not mean all aloof horses will crib.

Bertha was so removed from reality that he was almost impossible to connect with. He was a nice enough horse — not mean at all, moderately talented for dressage, a rather nondescript grayish white in color. Yet there was such a disconnect about him that he was often frustrating to ride. If the rider's aids were not perfectly timed and definite, with no mixed signals, Bertha would just hang on the rein and trudge along with a glazed look in his eyes.

Because of these training issues, either my husband or I rode him through the performance each evening. Even for us it was a difficult ride, because he did not respond quickly enough or often enough to the straightening or suppling aids. Most evenings as we proceeded through the drill in sitting trot, his back felt more like a bag of rocks than the supple, swinging back of an FEI horse.

Bertha lived in his own little world. He didn't keep up with any of the comings and goings along the barn aisle; in fact, the only thing he paid attention to was feed time. He had no equine friends and he was never the favorite of any of his grooms. A white horse that seemed to enjoy making himself filthy every day, he tolerated, rather than relished, the lengthy effort it took to transform him into a sparkling white steed for his nightly performance.

Bertha did not inspire anyone to do more with him than had to be done, and I think he liked it best that way. He was quite lazy and never gave any movement, either in the barn aisle or under saddle, one more iota of energy than was necessary in order to be left alone again. (This is more the exception than the rule for those higher on the aggressivity scale.) Keeping him both attentive and active was at times an impossible chore.

Ultimately, he was not much fun to ride because along with his aloofness and laziness, he was only moderately talented as a dressage horse. Bertha would have made a very tolerant lower-level lesson horse and may have been more suited for that purpose.

Horses like Bertha, especially in a busy training barn, can be much too easy to ignore. As a training strategy, however, it is far better to make such a horse interact with you as often as possible. This can be both time-consuming and unrewarding, but if you really want to make an aloof horse interactive, you must begin activities that get a response in the barn and carry the efforts through to your riding work. Since we had more than sixty-five horses and twenty-seven riders to deal with and organize each day, Bertha did not benefit from this particular strategy, at least not in the five years that I worked there. We were just too busy, and consequently Bertha rewarded himself by doing just enough to get by.

I have noticed that about 90 percent of the Lippizzans I have had the opportunity to study or spend time around were of an aloof or aloof-mix personality. Bertha, however, was the most aggressively aloof of them all.

*Pluto Bertha, the third horse from the right, performing
in the Arabian Nights Dinner Theater.*

CONCLUSIONS

Bertha was an easy horse to forget because he did little to define
or separate himself from the many other equine performers at
the Dinner Theater. Actually, his very nondescriptness helped me
define him as an aloof horse. Here are five of the clues:

1) He was so aggressively aloof that you could almost
   imagine him in a walking coma.

2) He rarely interacted with anything or anyone, whether
   equine or human.

3) He did not respond promptly to any request.

4) His cribbing behavior was characteristic of, though not
   exclusive to, the aloof type.

5) He showed very few personality traits at all.

CHAPTER SIX

THE CHALLENGING HORSE

THE CHALLENGING HORSE IS INTERACTIVE, but not necessarily in the same ways that a social horse is. From birth on, a challenging horse will test his surroundings and atmosphere, rather than just explore them. In fact, an aggressively challenging horse can be the bully of the pasture and should be monitored when introduced to a new horse in order to avoid injuries.

While challenging horses might display angry-type behavior more often than the other types do, they are not angry horses. They like to test and push their boundaries, but they do it in a matter-of-fact way. Challenging-type horses are the least naturally submissive of all of the types, but the majority of them learn, with the right kind of training and handling, that they need to promptly answer all requests from their handler or trainer. A horse with a challenging personality may need a firm hand at times but never benefits from an unfair one.

The old saying "Give him an inch and he'll take a mile" sums up an aggressively challenging personality. The pecking order between rider/trainer/handler and a challenging-type horse must be clearly defined early in the relationship and periodically refreshed in order to avoid such an individual stepping out of his boundaries and into yours. When someone describes her horse as argumentative, rebellious, or extremely bold, she is most likely talking about a challenging type. Both my husband and I have enjoyed success with a number of challenging-type horses because we have learned over the years how to handle them properly based on their character requirements.

Challenging horses can successfully participate in many or all equine activities, but I have observed them to be especially suited to certain sports. Racing, jumping, eventing, and many working cow horse sports are among the disciplines at which challenging-type horses excel.

CASE STUDY: *Chimon*

PASSIVE · · · · · · · · · AGGRESSIVE

| 1 | 2 | 3 | 4 | 5 | 6 | 7 | 8 | 9 | 10 |

passively challenging

A few years ago we imported a six-year-old Swedish Warmblood gelding from overseas. A colleague, just back from a buying trip to Sweden, caught up with us at a horse show in Indiana, eager to tell us about the sale horses that had captured her eye and her video lens over there. One night after the competition we had a glass of wine and looked at the prospects on the videotape. A client of ours was rather casually looking for a new project, not sure if he wanted a horse for himself or a talented resale investment. Horse number six on the thirteen-character videotape caught my interest.

Chimon was a son of the chestnut Swedish Warmblood stallion Amiral. (The famous dressage rider, trainer, and Olympian Kyra Kyrklund had successfully ridden Amiral to much international acclaim at the Grand Prix level.) I liked Chimon's extravagant and animated way of moving, but even on the carefully edited videotape we were watching, I could also see that there were some training —

Chimon poses with me at Paxton Farms.

and maybe some personality — issues. For example, when the demonstration rider asked for a movement that challenged Chimon's capabilities, he would visibly tighten himself up, then raise or lower his neck in an effort to change the subject. Soon a new clip would appear on the screen. What the untouched footage did show was movement of a very high quality but a little tight and a little behind the leg (not going freely forward from light leg pressure).

Being the overconfident, enthusiastic, optimistic sort that I was back then, I glossed over the obvious training or character issues and focused only on the potential I had observed. I wanted the horse in my barn; he looked talented and fun to work with. I informed the prospective buyer that the number six horse was the one to bring over.

Negotiations were completed and over he came. I met him as he stepped off the trailer from New York, following his flight from Sweden. He was rather plain when standing still: cute, but not as

CHALLENGING
PERSONALITY CHARACTERISTICS

▶ *Interaction.* Strong sense of self: may seem prideful or arrogant. Stallions of this personality are generally more aggressive than stallions of other types.

▶ *Need for personal space.* Guarded or somewhat territorial about their personal space. Must be taught quite early not to invade their handlers' personal space.

▶ *Relationship to herd/humans.* Usually near the top of the pecking order. Need constant clarification of their place in the horse-trainer relationship.

▶ *Adaptability.* Initially resistant to new suggestions.

▶ *Reactivity.* Prone to more explosive reactions.

▶ *Response to aids.* Confrontational about stimuli or aids.

▶ *Fight or flight?* More fight than flight tendencies.

▶ *Behavior quirks.* When young, and even into adulthood, may exhibit threatening behavior such as biting, kicking, charging, or rushing.

▶ *Opportunism.* Opportunistic: quickly spot and exploit opportunities provided by timid or inexperienced riders.

▶ *Response to training.* When properly trained make reliable, confident partners.

▶ *Often strong, brave performers* with a certain charisma.

▶ *Happiest & most content* when having things their own way.

▶ *Breeds that may be associated with challenging-type personalities:* Swedish Warmbloods, some Thoroughbreds, many small ponies.

impressive as he had been on the videotape; a more "orange" than chestnut-colored 16-hand horse with a pony face and a deceptively quiet, confident, and somewhat tranquil demeanor. I liked him immediately. (I should probably quit saying that, because I like most horses immediately. I would be better off to mention the horses I don't like, but so far I haven't found any.)

Chimon settled into his new stall and atmosphere with relative ease. I began to wonder if the testy behavior I had seen on the videotape was just evidence of some unresolved training issues and not an indication of his character at all. It is important when you meet a new horse not to rush toward any quick personality assessments, especially with the more passive types. A more passive-type character will be harder to read and may take days or weeks to define correctly, especially if you are new to this practice. Remember that geldings (because of their lack of hormones) will be more passive in expressing a personality type than either stallions or mares. And Chimon was very interested in his environment. If I had used only the information I had gathered in handling him on the ground and disregarded what I had seen on the videotape, I might have leaned toward categorizing him as a passively social type.

My first challenging-type clue came when I turned him out with our resident nice guy, a passively social horse who refused to argue with anyone, be he man or beast. Chimon took immediate charge of Jasper and started herding him around the pasture, making sure he understood who was the leader in their herd of two. It was evident by Chimon's behavior that he was much more interested in bossing Jasper than he was in just socializing with him. He didn't hurt the young gelding, but his behavior put me on alert.

*Chimon and I competing,
Dressage at Devon.*

Over the next few days Chimon more positively identified himself as a passively challenging type who was quiet and hard to read
in the stable, but clearer under saddle or in turnout. When I took a
soft rein contact in the bridle, his first instinct was to lean on it, and
if I laid my leg on his side he would push against it almost reflexively. Hollow on his left side and stiff on his right, he objected, first
quietly and then more strenuously, when I tried to work on some
suppling and straightening exercises. When a challenging horse is
pressured, arguing becomes an easy option. I tried to steer clear of
the argument but still accomplish my training goals.

Overall, Chimon proved to be quite passive in expressing his
challenging disposition. With clear aids and my quiet but firm
resolve that he should answer every request promptly, he made
rapid progress up the dressage ladder. As well as talented, athletic,
and very energetic, he was supremely confident, another trait challenging and social horses share. These attributes all contributed to
the good test marks and positive comments Chimon received from
many different judges during his first season with us.

KEEPING A CHALLENGING HORSE ON TRACK

The most important thing to keep in mind when working with all horses, but especially those of a challenging nature, is that it is never wise to go "into the argument" that a horse brings to the table. Rather, it is imperative that the horse continually be guided toward the solution with clear and at times firm aids that are consistent time and again.

For example, if you are working on a shoulder-in and the horse starts to grab the bit and take you off your intended line of travel, you must continue to reestablish both the position (shoulder-in) and your line in order to stay on track and make progress. The horse must not be allowed to change the subject. Just make sure that you do not introduce something that the horse is not physically or mentally capable of responding to at that time.

Only on a few occasions while training with me did his behavior escalate upwards into more aggressively challenging actions. (Luckily for me these rare fits of temper were short-lived, because he had a heck of an athletic buck on him.) Three times during the course of our two-and–a-half-year partnership he managed to unload me over differences of opinion about various training issues. He always ended up conforming to my requests, though, and eventually evolved into a hard-working and very reliable partner.

When he arrived from Sweden, he could not have put together a Second Level test. A year later, he won the Prix St. Georges in a class of more than forty at the prestigious Dressage at Devon in Pennsylvania. After winning a number of United States Dressage Federation (USDF) Regional Championships and a USDF Horse of the Year title, Chimon made the list of the top twelve Intermediate horses in the country and qualified for the United States Equestrian Team's Festival of Champions in Gladstone, New Jersey.

During the two and a half years I had Chimon in training, he became a wonderful and trustworthy show partner — brave, hardworking, opinionated, and confident. He was my original "Lion King Horse", with a costumed dressage exhibition that became so popular I had to transfer the act to another horse after he left.

CONCLUSIONS

Because he was quite passive about his personality traits, Chimon was more difficult to read when I first met him. The first clues on the videotape were subtle, but it wasn't until he was turned out with another horse in our field at home that I spotted the first clear signs of challenging-type behavior. Here are three of the clues I observed:

1) In a turnout situation Chimon was clearly bent on herding and bossing the other horse in the field.

2) Under saddle, his body tensed and resisted my aids.

3) Confident in most situations, Chimon had some strong opinions, which he did not mind sharing with me, especially in a training situation.

CASE STUDY: *Stormy Pursuit*

I had worked with Standardbred racehorses for about three years when I met jet-black Stormy Pursuit. Charlie Clark, one of the old-time "speed trainers" of the racing world, had been in charge of her two-year-old career. He said she was amazingly fast, but could be ill-tempered and was hard to keep sound.

Stormy entered our training stable at the end of her two-year-old racing season. For readers not familiar with the training work and strenuous physical regimen that young racehorses are exposed to, a long (late into her two-year-old season) two-year-old race-horse has more wear and tear on her than most five- or six-year-olds in many other disciplines. The 15.3-hand filly was ragged, tired, and cranky. Her conformation (bench-kneed and pigeon-toed) was not ideally suited for such speed, so consequently she had put a lot of strain on her front ankles. She was sore and sour, and she didn't mind letting everybody know about it.

My first assignment was to get her sound enough to race. I have learned a lot about lameness from my years on the racetrack and am grateful for that knowledge (although not happy that it had to come from so many young and injured racehorses). The track is famous for its iodine paints, astringent liniments, heat rubs, and clay poultices — old and new potions, all claiming to help any horse get back to racing soundness in world-record time.

Keeping a horse healthy and sound enough to race is not really about any of that stuff, however. It is about paying attention. That includes monitoring the legs, feet, digestion, and health of your horse and not letting anything go unnoticed or get out of hand. Stormy's sore and swollen front ankles needed constant care. Ice boots, cold-water wraps, heat liniments, and stable bandages were the order of the day, with carefully applied elastic support bandages every time she went on the track to work.

Within a few weeks of such diligent care, her seemingly permanent bad mood began to dissipate. She was still a challenging mare (she had strong opinions and a decidedly testy attitude); she just wasn't as angry about being sore anymore.

Keeping a horse healthy and sound enough to race

is really about paying attention.

Stormy was very territorial about her stall with anyone but me. I could be in her stall grooming her or working on her legs and she wouldn't even have a halter on. If someone approached her doorway, on the other hand, or tried to enter her stall, she would charge them with pinned ears and gnashing teeth. Many a full-grown man would retreat hastily under that sort of attack. She could be quite evil-looking, and she rather enjoyed intimidating people and other horses when they passed by her stall.

When Stormy tried out some of this attitude on me early in our relationship, I had held my ground and set her down — that is, I made sure she knew I was the leader in our herd of two. A few

Stormy Pursuit racing at "The Red Mile," Lexington, Kentucky.

times I had to give her an open-handed slap under her belly as I stood beside her to harness her. From then on I had her respect.

People who had witnessed her behavior around other people and then saw how she interacted with me thought that she loved me and was attached to me. She didn't, and she wasn't; she just respected me. She probably did like me a little because I took care of her sore legs and I fed her every day. No matter what personality type you are working with, if you bring food, you are the local hero in any stable. Challenging horses keep track of things like that and are always ready to test newcomers. They will even try to threaten the people that feed them, but if you stand your ground they will concede. Remember, you get what you settle for in most equine relationships, so don't settle for bad behavior.

Quick and as tough as nails out on the track, Stormy understood racing and she wanted to win, as long as it was on her terms. She was not a come-from-behind horse; she wanted to race out front, where she could look her competition in the eye and dare them to try to pass her. If she didn't get away in front of the pack within the first eighth of a mile, she would jump it off. This is a racetrack term for a Standardbred that quits trying on purpose, deliberately breaking out of the trot or pace gait into a gallop. When a Standard-bred breaks gait, the driver has to take back to correct the situation, losing much ground in the process. If Stormy's driver pushed her too hard, on the other hand, or used the whip indiscriminately, she would pin her ears angrily and back into him, threatening to kick him out of the sulky if he did not desist.

She would not be dictated to out on the racetrack. Consequently, she finished either first or last in almost every race we entered her in. Stormy knew how she wanted things (her way) and there was no middle ground.

She would not be dictated to out on the racetrack. Consequently, she finished either first or last in almost every race we entered her in.

During her three-year-old year, Stormy set three track records, and she won more than $100,000 racing. She time-trialed that year in Lexington, Kentucky, as the tenth fastest mare in history up to that date with a time of 1:53.1 for the mile, extremely fast back in 1985.

Her career suited her personality more than it suited her conformation. She was a headstrong and memorable horse and I think she could have excelled at many other disciplines had she received the training for them. She had a powerful engine and was lightning fast and as tough-minded as any horse I had ever met. I'm sure that with the right handling and training she could have done a lot of things well. She was a tremendous athlete who earned my complete respect far more easily than I earned hers.

CONCLUSIONS

Stormy defined herself as a challenging type via the following behavior signals:

1) She exhibited testy and threatening behavior toward just about everyone.

2) She was territorial about her personal space, a common trait among challenging-type horses.

3) She was a very confident mare. She understood what racing was and she wanted to win, but on her terms.

4) While I was clearly her favorite person, I never had the feeling that she really liked me (she seemed too independent for that), but after I had earned her respect she quit trying to test me.

I would have rated her at a 6 or 7 on the passive-aggressive scale in regard to her challenging characteristics.

CASE STUDY: *Marcel*

PASSIVE   AGGRESSIVE

| 1 | 2 | 3 | 4 | 5 | 6 | 7 | 8 | 9 | 10 |

aggressively challenging

Marcel was a five-year-old imported Swedish Warmblood stallion when my husband and I first met him in 1998, before we moved up to Illinois from the Dinner Theater in Orlando. Owned by Bob Oury, he was one of five stallions we would be responsible for training should we choose to make the move. When we first observed the beautiful dark bay young stallion, he was standing in his stall with one front leg bandaged and a cheeky look on his face. He was on fabricated lay-up, being masqueraded as a lame horse by his trainer, who was afraid to handle or ride him.

Kim, who speaks excellent Spanish, questioned the young Mexican groom, Oscar, about the injury, and the young man grinned and said, "Nothing. I'm just supposed to keep one of his legs wrapped up so the trainer can tell everyone he is lame." He laughed and added, "I wrap a different one every other day." We removed the bandage, examined the horse's cool, tight, and unblemished leg, and asked Oscar to turn him out in the stallion pen so we could watch him move.

After dragging the groom over to two other stallions' stalls to fight with them over their gates, then walking out to the paddock on his hind legs, Marcel finally allowed Oscar to turn him loose. Definitely not lame, he tore around the stallion pen as if he were auditioning for the equine *King Kong*. On that initial viewing he looked exactly like what he would later define himself as: a willful, arrogant, and aggressively challenging young stallion.

Not only was Marcel not lame, but he was barely able to be handled. In fact he was familiar with the idea of training because he had been training everyone to put up with his misbehaviors for a very long time. It is not a good idea for any young stallion to realize how strong and unruly he can be, because it is difficult for him to give up his very real sense of power once he has gained it. Marcel was clear proof of that. He had no respect for any procedure or person that might attempt to influence his behavior, and because he was so huge he could be very threatening.

Bob indulged in a herd-type breeding system when we first met him, and while you may assume an aggressively challenging stallion might be more suited to pasture breeding than the other types, you would be wrong. Marcel was constantly in trouble, getting kicked and set down by the older mares, who rightly wondered what kind of inexperienced idiot would try to run a group of older broodmares around as if it were his right. True to his nature, though, and despite several injuries, Marcel could not be content with any lesser role than king of the herd. The mares took turns setting him in his place, a place where his aggressively challenging personality refused to stay. In stark contrast, another stallion, a passively social type named Liberty, had gladly allowed the boss mare to stay in charge and was happily socializing and mingling with his small harem without injury or disruption.

Marcel was difficult to train under saddle because he had already been started with disastrous results. He had no respect for process or people and he actually wanted (and knew how) to get rid of a rider attempting to mount his 17-hand back. Unfortunately for us, he was both clever and athletic enough to do it. Trying to bite you while you mounted, rearing, spinning, running you into the barn, attacking other horses while under saddle: these were common practices for the wily youngster. He seemed to live to argue, and controversy resulted from almost any request, regardless of how simple.

Eventually my husband got Marcel broke enough to go to a few horse shows, and for the small amount of time that he did behave in the dressage arena he scored very high marks because he was so beautiful and such a good mover. In the end, however, he was too unpredictable about behaving to do well as a competition horse. His strong, hormone-charged nature suggested that any and all requests were worth arguing about. It became pointless for us to continue with him in the sport of dressage, which is made up of so many small requests that must be responded to without question.

Kim started working Marcel "at liberty," the art of working a horse loose in the arena, having him respond to whip signals and body language in order to obey. Marcel was very suited to this work. Kim started the process in the round pen, and because answering the aids still allowed Marcel freedom in the arena without direct contact, his desire to argue was somewhat disarmed. Before long, Marcel was working in a full-sized ring, where his wild and somewhat cheeky responses to Kim's aids only made him that much more glorious and inspiring to watch. Marcel is now a fairly accomplished exhibition horse and has twice been a featured solo act in the Pfizer Fantasia, a nighttime extravaganza held in conjunction with the Equine Affaire in both Ohio and Massachusetts.

Do not forget that aggressively challenging horses will go to great lengths to initiate misbehavior, to the point that they might endanger or injure themselves or others in the process. Even after they are trained, this needs to be remembered and respected.

CONCLUSIONS

It was not hard to diagnose Marcel as an aggressively challenging individual, and here were four of the clues:

1) He had extreme, often dangerous misbehaviors (from trying to bite a person mounting him to attacking other horses) and a very willful attitude.

2) He resisted almost every rider request.

3) In a herd-breeding situation he was always in trouble as he tried to boss the mares and they repeatedly set him down.

4) His sheer size and strength, along with the lack of respect he had developed for people in his early handling, made him a dangerous prospect to work with.

If Marcel had been started in a very clear and structured environment he may have been salvageable as both a competition horse and a breeding stallion. But he was not. He remained a stallion until the age of twelve. He blatantly and intentionally injured his owner while being handled around some mares one day and was gelded not long after. Gelding will have only a minimal effect on a horse such as this. In my opinion Marcel was not successful as a stallion, because unfortunately his challenging temperament was passed on to the majority of his foals.

PART THREE

MIXED
PERSONALITIES

A detailed look at each

of the mixed horse personality types

with individual case studies

A mixed personality is evident when a horse appears to be of one personality type but occasionally seems to borrow behaviors from another type, often when under stress. His most observable and easily defined characteristics remain his dominant type, while his "borrowed behaviors" serve in more of a secondary or auxiliary function. With a mixed personality, it is most effective to train with the horse's basic or dominant personality in mind.

CHAPTER SEVEN

THE SOCIAL MIX

THE SOCIAL-MIX HORSE is still basically a social type who, under stress, conflict, or a change of environment, repeatedly displays discernible traits from one of the other personality groups. The possible mixes are social-fearful, social-aloof, and social-challenging.

To avoid making the personality mixes too complicated, I have listed each combination with the dominant type first. A horse will usually spend most of his time, especially when comfortable, displaying the dominant aspects of his personality. His auxiliary personality traits may be observable only under stressful situations or if he is off guard or out of his comfort range. A wise horse trainer needs to become familiar with and appreciative of individual horses' characteristics and train accordingly.

The Social-Fearful Mix

The social-fearful horse is an engaging yet watchful character whose comfort range is somewhat narrower than that of a horse with strictly social characteristics. When things are well in this horse's world, he will resemble any other social horse, but when stress or conflict arises, he will display fearful-type behavior. He will need to be reassured, not punished, until he regains his composure and confidence. This type of horse will bond best with a fair-minded but empathetic handler or rider.

CASE STUDY: *Quebec*

passively to moderately social

PASSIVE	1	2	3	4	5	6	7	8	9	10	AGGRESSIVE

aggressively fearful

You may suspect during the course of this book that I have a lot of favorite horses, and that would be true. I love horses, and I have many treasured equine friends. I do not view this as sappy or sentimental; in fact, I consider myself a clear-headed and extremely pragmatic individual. I see horses for who and what they are, and because of that I have formed some keen attachments to them. That being said, my all-time favorite horse, the one who owns the biggest piece of my ever-expanding heart, is a silver-gray Arabian stallion with a social-fearful personality.

I met Quebec shortly after I began working at the Arabian Nights Dinner Theater in Orlando. As the new recruit, I was frequently sent to the back barn or quarantine barn to take care of the four to six horses that were stabled there. This barn was a short-term residence for any horses coming into or leaving the facility. New arrivals would spend thirty days there to be sure they would not bring any infectious maladies into the barn that might jeopardize our equine stars' abilities to perform.

Quebec was a six-year-old silver-gray Arabian with an exceptionally beautiful head and eye. He was stabled in the back barn, waiting to leave the facility for good. He had been tried out for the dinner show but had yet to find a niche into which he fit. In the opinions of several top trainers he was a very athletic and talented

Quebec and I,
just after winning
a regional championship
qualifier in Perry,
Georgia, in 1995.

horse, but too nervous under pressure to be suitable for any rigorous or top-level competitive work.

He didn't seem very nervous to me when I went in to introduce myself. In fact, he was the kind of horse that made you feel badly if you walked by him or took care of him without some sort of interaction. He liked the attention and was very interested in me. Within a few days I found myself volunteering for all of the duties back there just so I could go say hi to the friendly fellow, groom him, or turn him out for a little while.

I asked Kim, who was then the head trainer, why such a fine-looking and personable horse had not made it into the show. "He's confused," Kim replied. "Some of his early training must have gone badly because he's a bit of a live wire under saddle. It will be too time-consuming for us to fix him, so he has to leave."

Wanting to ride the young stallion myself, I made my way to the owner's office to request permission. When I offered to ride

Quebec on my own time, he found no reason to dissuade me. "You can ride him for a few days if you want," he told me, "but he is still leaving in two weeks." Our daily routine was that work started at twelve-thirty each afternoon, and dinner break lasted from half-past four until six o'clock, when everyone would return to prepare for that evening's performance. Dinner break was my opportunity: as soon as my afternoon duties were finished, I fairly pranced out to the back barn to collect Quebec for our first ride.

He was feeling rather fresh as we made our way toward the main barn. He jumped around on the end of his leadrope, then looked warily at me to see if he was in trouble. I petted his neck and talked to him the whole way. When we approached the tacking area his whole demeanor changed. He became quiet and withdrawn, and when I tied him and went to get some tack, he started to sweat.

Racehorses will often sweat profusely in nervous anticipation of a race. The racetrack term for this is washing out. Not all racehorses behave this way, but many fearful ones will. The entire body becomes covered in sweat despite little or no exertion.

Quebec started washing out before I even had the saddle on. He had turned inward and become quiet and withdrawn. He appeared to be in a frozen state of panic, and I wished for the thousandth time that horses could more clearly tell us about their pasts.

Sensing he was on the edge of a meltdown, I governed my actions accordingly, carrying on slowly and quietly, talking to him all the while. After he was bridled I led him out to the arena. I decided against longeing him, figuring his problems had nothing to do with extra energy and would best be solved under saddle.

Most fearful horses are rarely offensive in their behavior. Almost everything they do is defensive or reflexive in its origin. I was not worried that Quebec would hurt me; in fact, he was far more worried about his situation than I was. He was just scared, not testy or threatening. If I did get hurt it would be because of my improper timing or handling, not as a direct result of his bad behavior. I led Quebec to the center of the arena, tightened his girth, adjusted my stirrups, and climbed on.

Quebec appeared to be in a frozen state of panic and I wished for the thousandth time that horses could more clearly tell us about their pasts.

As soon as I was aboard, Quebec held his breath, raised and tightened his whole neck, and started prancing wildly. His back felt like a rock. Since nothing good could come of such tension, I softened the reins so he knew I would not try to restrain him — having retracted his neck he was behind the influence of the bit anyway — and urged him forward. He shot off in an almost hysterical gallop as if he were being chased by demons. I could have been anybody or nobody on his back for all the attention he paid me. I centered myself, sat quietly, and let him run.

The indoor arena at Arabian Nights is a fine place to let a nervous horse run off some tension. The footing is fairly secure, the walls and curtains don't invite jumping out, and the whole place is climate-controlled. As Quebec ran, I made small movements to help him balance in the corners, but other than that I continued to sit quietly and wait for him to relax just a little bit.

Round and round we went: Quebec, with his head up, eyes wild, nostrils flaring; me, sitting quietly in forward seat with a relaxed rein, petting his neck and talking to him. Quebec had still not acknowledged me, he was somewhere far away, but I continued talking to him as he raced around the arena and occasionally slid on the Fibar footing.

On the third day I felt him change.

Eventually I spiraled him into a smaller and smaller circle until he slowed down and then stopped. As soon as we were standing still, he started to fidget and act as if he wanted to take off again, so I dismounted and took him back to the barn to bathe and walk him. Kim found me at about a quarter to six, out in the back barn putting Quebec away, and inquired about my progress. "Didn't make any," I replied, "but I'm not done trying."

The second ride was a duplicate of the first, but on the third day, about ten minutes into the run, I felt him change. He put an ear on me and started to slow down on his own. I let my hands find his mouth, and he sped up briefly, only to slow down again on the next lap. This time he let my hands stay with him and continued to slow down on his own while keeping his left ear and eye turned to me. He slowed to a walk, and I petted him and dismounted.

The next day, the fearful horse was absent. The social horse I had originally met out in the back barn was the horse that showed up for our ride. The newly composed stallion barely sweated as I tacked him, and when I mounted up he waited almost calmly while I sat still and petted his neck. I took a feel of his mouth and he walked quietly forward into my hands. I kept the ride short, worked on some minor steering issues, and praised him lavishly afterward.

It was over. Whatever had happened to him early on to make him so panicky was behind him. Now he could be trained. As soon as our relationship under saddle was established, Quebec's social self came forward and he became almost slavish in his desire to learn and to work. I have never, before or since, worked with a horse that learned things so quickly and paid such rapt attention to his lessons. About a week after I had began with Quebec, Kim stayed back during his lunch hour to observe our progress. He was both amazed and impressed. He agreed to back me when I asked Mark to let Quebec stay and prepare for a career in showbiz.

Permission was granted and Quebec became my Dinner Theater partner. I trained and rode him in the Opening Act, The Bedouin Drill, The Square Dance, and The Flag Drill, a high-speed Western act done at a gallop with four riders carrying American flags. We also worked on the dressage movements that would prepare him for the Pas de Deux, the Dancing Horses of the Desert, and a solo spot in The Latin Act.

I was so proud of Quebec that I asked for and received permission to enter him in some Open Dressage competitions, starting at Fourth Level, less than a year after our initial ride. He qualified for and then won the Reserve National Championship at the Arabian Nationals, his first year in competition. We continued to train, and the next year Quebec was a respectable competitor at the Prix St. Georges and Intermediate I levels in open FEI competitions on the tough Florida circuit. During this time he received the scores that would qualify him as the first purebred Arabian stallion in the country to be approved as a Trakehner breeding stallion.

Quebec is an example of why it is so important to look beyond the obvious behavior or even misbehavior of any horse.

Around that time I received a phone call from Kathie Cox, the director of The Mane Event, a nighttime equine extravaganza held during USA's Equitana in Lexington, Kentucky. She asked if I had anything fabulous that would do as a finale for the three-night performance. With only an idea to back me up, I volunteered Quebec to do a Grand Prix bridleless exhibition that would include fifteen loose horses running around in the arena as we performed.

Quebec rose to the occasion. The first day without a bridle he figured out how to do all of his FEI movements without any rein aids. I used a neck rope on him, and since there are always seat and leg aids to accompany every movement, Quebec made educated guesses as to what I wanted from him.

It worked: the show went beautifully. Mark had suggested I use Arabian costuming and music for the act, creating a haunting, almost mystical background for our movements. On the rehearsal night Quebec was a little nervous about the environment. He was not panicky, however, and he let me guide him through the routine with minimal fuss. He bloomed a little more each night, so that by Saturday evening's sold-out performance he was downright comfortable out there.

Who would have believed that the panicky horse I had mounted for the first time less than three-and-a-half years earlier could evolve into the attentive, composed stallion that performed so easily in front of an audience of ten thousand?

Along with being my favorite horse and training project to date, Quebec is an example of why it is so important to look beyond the obvious behavior or even misbehavior of any horse. It is possible that he has just been waiting. Waiting for someone to see who he is, not just how he acts, and to find a way to communicate with him in a voice he can relate to.

CONCLUSIONS

Quebec was a magnificent horse with some confusion and fear issues when under saddle that masked his true character. He was always wonderful to work with on the ground.

When I met him I would have rated his social side at about a 4 and his fearful behavior (when he displayed it) at about a 9. Over time, all fearful behavior disappeared in his daily work, and only small hints would show up under stressful situations.

Quebec is an excellent example of a horse who needed and thrived on a one-on-one partnership situation.

The Social-Aloof Mix

At first glance, a social-aloof horse might seem a bit of an oxymoron, and if I were to suggest that a horse might act both social and aloof at the same time, there may be cause for some doubt. As I stated earlier, mixed personalities are slightly more complicated both to read and to deal with.

A horse of any personality type who appears at times to borrow behaviors from another personality is probably a mix. If a horse is a social-aloof type, his social character is dominant much of the time, but under stress, conflict, or a change in environment he may display some aloof tendencies. Some examples may clarify.

CASE STUDY: *San Remo*

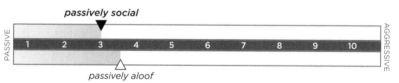

passively social

PASSIVE 1 2 3 4 5 6 7 8 9 10 AGGRESSIVE

passively aloof

A few years ago, some clients of ours imported a wonderful Hanoverian gelding from Germany, who was late into his fourth year. A beautiful dark bay, he had an appealing and affable nature. It had been my experience that many Hanoverians are aloof by nature, so I was pleasantly surprised to introduce myself to this passively social young gelding.

San Remo was a beautiful and talented young individual with huge strong gaits and a wonderful work ethic, which makes for a rewarding training project. The only riding issues I found were that he was somewhat stiff and crooked with his right side. No worries: there are plenty of exercises to fix such problems. I took

TESTING THE LIMITS

At times during any training process you will find the edge, or limit, of your equine charge's physical or mental capabilities. Since these limits change and broaden as the horse strengthens and matures, you must be ready to change your expectations, depending on the circumstances. Your actions during these times of pressure or stress will play a large part in defining you as a rider or trainer.

In addition, the way your horse reacts or responds during these moments of stress or conflict will help define or clarify his personality for you. Try to stay aware of what is happening and pay close attention to the details of these interactions. Think clearly and try to classify the information you receive from your horse.

QUESTIONS TO ASK

▶ What does your horse do when the work becomes more difficult or tiring? Does he grow quieter, more explosive, flighty, or testy?

▶ How does he respond to your corrections and interactions? Do they make him afraid, belligerent, dull, or distracted?

San Remo and myself: high score of show, Wellington, Florida 2001.

San Remo to Florida that winter with the rest of my show string to prepare him for the FEI five-year-old dressage tests and the North American Championships the following spring.

Normally, if I used clear, well-timed aids, San Remo was happy to respond in a predictable manner. Whenever I hit a sticky patch with him, however, he would zone out a bit, tuning out stimuli and seeming to withdraw from the lesson. When he was stressed, for example, or if I moved the intensity of the work up too quickly, he would stall out and appear almost balky, avoiding even the easier responses that he was already familiar with.

Because this was uncharacteristic of him, I soon learned to back off and assess the situation before proceeding. A couple of times I made the mistake of just adding more pressure to the situation, but because San Remo was already out of his comfort range I did not get my desired result. If I retreated toward easier work that he could understand and succeed at, both his confidence and his good humor would soon return.

I noted another clue to San Remo's personality when I turned him out to relax and play with a pair of social horses, one passively and one more aggressively social. While he appeared to enjoy their company at first, eventually they overstimulated him with their constant interactions. They weren't mean or harmful; they just overwhelmed him, until he retreated to a corner and stood with his butt to them, blocking them out. I went out and rescued him and thereafter turned him out beside and not with the same two horses, a situation that suited him better. He could interact with them over the fence and then withdraw whenever he chose to.

San Remo went on to win the five-year-old FEI qualifier for dressage horses and became the only horse in North America that year to qualify for the World Championships in Verden, Germany. For the remaining time that he was in my stable and under my care he continued to define himself as a passively social horse with aloof tendencies that showed up under pressure or stress.

CONCLUSIONS

San Remo was a fairly uncomplicated project. He had been well started, was suited for his intended discipline, and ranked at about a 3 on the aggressivity scale in terms of his social personality. When he retreated toward aloof behavior, I did not just turn up the heat with my aids and continue to train him in his aloof mode. I have made that mistake before, and although progress may have been made in those circumstances, it is always best to train any horse with his basic or dominant personality in mind and on display. When a horse is not in his dominant or most trainable state his association with the work may be somewhat compromised.

The Social-Challenging Mix

Some of my favorite horses have been of a social-challenging nature. These types are usually interested in their surroundings and almost always interacting with it in some way or another. They differ from the purely social horse in that when they get stressed or pushed too hard, they are more likely to push back or make a definite and clearly readable effort to make themselves comfortable again.

CASE STUDY: *Diablo*

Diablo, a dark bay blanket Appaloosa, was a recently gelded eight-year-old when I first met him in Eustis, Florida. I met his owner Sally on the same day, and she became one of my very dear friends. Sally was a farm woman, a big, strong, bale-your-own-hay, run-your-own-back-hoe, butcher-your-own-hogs kind of farm woman. She had a loud, laughing voice, strong manly hands, and a matter-of-fact way of fixing and handling everything. Everything, that is, except Diablo.

Diablo did not want to be thought of as a farm animal at all. He wanted to be Sally's companion or her pet, not her transportation or entertainment on team-penning night. A very clever horse, he spent a lot of time trying to get his owner to interact with him, efforts that were largely wasted on her. She just wanted him to behave and obey. Had Diablo been an aloof horse, the situation would probably have been fine for both of them.

Since I was the new big-shot, fix-all-the-problem-horses-in-the-area trainer, she asked if I would take a stab at redeeming Diablo. Currently they were arguing about barrel racing. She complained that as soon as Diablo saw that there were barrels in the arena he would just grab the bit and take off at a mad gallop. There was no stopping, no steering, nothing. I told Sally to bring Diablo and his barrels down and to give me a few days with him.

The next day we set up the barrels in an arena in my front field and I mounted Diablo for the first time. Sure enough, he started hopping and prancing about, trying to grab the bit and take off. When I did not pull back on the reins he threw his head up in the air and dashed off, just begging me to try and steer him. I did not cooperate but let him run off with his head in the air; in fact, once I got a feel for his movement, I encouraged him to run faster than he wanted. I did not argue with him at all.

Since the arena was fenced, and I knew his actions were deliberate and not panicky or fearful, I just let him run. As soon as I eliminated the bridle argument, which was Diablo's only means of taking control of the situation, he started to look to me for direction. When I made him run faster without pulling on his face, he began trying to slow down. I petted him and talked to him while he ran and pretty soon he dropped his head and slowed down completely. He had forgotten about the barrels altogether.

Diablo wanted the interaction of a one-on-one relationship, and he needed his rider to stay in the game with him and interact accordingly. When this didn't happen, his challenging side came forth, and he tried to take control of his rides by misbehaving. By choosing not to join this argument I avoided having to deal with his challenging-type behavior head on.

Because his dominant side was not of a challenging nature, he soon returned to more interactive and less controlling behavior. When I did not jump into his problem with him he realized the argument was not necessary in the first place. Our conclusion was that Sally needed to interact with Diablo when things were going well, not just when he was wrong or she wanted something new.

Diablo's behavioral problems sorted themselves out in short order. He actually liked the training process and was willing to try almost any activity. Less than a year later, at Sally's insistence, I entered him in the Battle of the Breeds Contest in Ocala, Florida. He first won the right to represent the Appaloosa breed and then went forward to compete against the chosen Arabian, Quarter Horse, Thoroughbred, Paso Fino, Morgan, and draft horse.

The one-day competition consisted of a 5/8-mile race, a barrel race, a hit-and-hurry jumping round, a trail class with a number of obstacles to negotiate, a driving course, and a "Champagne Class." In this class all of the competitors had to ride at three different paces with a full glass of champagne in their hands. The rider with the most liquid left in the glass at the end won.

Diablo and I won the Champagne Class and the jumping round. We were second in the barrel race and third in the 5/8-mile race and the driving class. Unfortunately, as many equine events do, this one ran two hours longer than the estimated time. Because I was working at the Arabian Nights Dinner Theater then, and scheduled to ride in almost every act that evening, I had to leave.

Diablo and I missed the final event, the trail class, and were consequently disqualified. Nevertheless, even without the last event, Diablo and I had earned more points than any other horse and rider combination. We would have won.

Unlike Sally, I really didn't mind. Diablo had behaved like a prince, he had learned a lot of new skills for that competition, and I was happy with everything he had accomplished.

Eventually Diablo moved over to the dinner show with me, where he learned to pull a burning wagon in the Indian Raid, ride in the complicated but fun square dance routine, and back up our first-string reining horse in the featured Native American Act.

CONCLUSIONS

Diablo was a great horse with loads of character. Like many social and challenging horses, he was quite confident by nature.

I rated him at about a 4 on the aggressivity scale in terms of his dominant social type and a 4 or 5 in terms of his auxiliary challenging-type personality whenever he expressed it. Unfortunately, prior to meeting me he had spent too much training time asserting himself in a challenging-type manner. Once we found a way to make progress within his dominant social type, he became much less volatile to deal with.

Even though both social and challenging horses enjoy interacting, there is usually a different motive behind challenging-type interactions, so they should not be handled in the same manner. Arguing with a horse is not an interaction, but a senseless waste of time. Try to avoid disagreements whenever you can. Focus instead on clear, understandable aids with expected answers.

CASE STUDY: *Don Bryn Ideal*

passively social

PASSIVE | AGGRESSIVE

| 1 | 2 | 3 | 4 | 5 | 6 | 7 | 8 | 9 | 10 |

passively challenging

I met Don Bryn Ideal when he was two and I was eighteen. Having recently finished high school, I was working at Greenwood Racetrack in Toronto, Canada. I had previously been employed as a groom in a large, competitive Standardbred training operation.

Along with their salaries, the grooms received a percentage of their charges' earnings, so the new hires got the castoffs. As the newest hire, I was given the horses least likely to succeed. Broken-down or untalented three year olds and untried two year olds without a pedigree behind them were the least likely to earn their grooms a bonus at the end of the year.

Don Bryn Ideal fell into the last category. Untried, and the first foal out of an indifferent race mare, he was hardly the talk of the barn aisle. He had already earned the nickname Shorty, for he was barely larger than a pony. He had a stout, block-shaped body, short, sturdy legs, and a thick, stocky neck. Even his coloring did not distinguish him in any way: an unimpressive mud brown without any white markings on legs or face to give him added character.

What was inspiring and noticeable about him was his great personality. As soon as I met him I looked into a face full of character and interest, and I thought, this guy wants to be somebody. I was happy to take him into my string, and very soon I was assigned to handle and drive him for his daily jog miles.

Shorty headed out to the training track each day as if he were the little engine that could. He liked working. Sitting behind him in the jog cart every morning, I felt the determination and purpose in his choppy little strides. During the first lap he might clown around a little bit if he was fresh or the weather was cool, but he was soon down to the business of working. Head down, legs churning like pistons, he rolled around the track looking for horses to pass, wait for, and then happily pass again.

Twice a week, John, the head trainer, would work him at speed, with the other colts his age. After about three weeks of training John handed Shorty back to me after one of his faster miles and winked. "This one's got some heart," he said admiringly. "He may make up for his size after all."

Shorty's biggest asset was that he was interested in racing and he wanted to be the one in front at the end of every training mile. He tried harder than the other colts did. He didn't mind being tired and he never lost his good humor. His training times kept improving, and by late spring he was ready for his first baby race.

He won. Two weeks later, he won again. By his second win he knew that he should turn into the winner's circle for his picture and the big fuss. His social side loved the attention, and he was just challenging enough to understand what his job was and to have the will to win.

One night, after three straight sire stakes wins, Shorty lost in a photo finish on a half-mile track in London, Ontario. The race was so close that even the tired and sweaty youngster thought he had won. On the way back to the barn I had to drag him past the winner's circle. He wanted to go in there for the big fuss. He was uncharacteristically miserable as I unharnessed and cooled him out that night.

The following week he left no doubt, winning by his largest margin ever and then fairly prancing back to the winner's circle for his photo. If horses can smile, then Shorty was laughing as he posed for his picture that night.

When the race year ended, we gave the horses a little vacation. Shorty's days consisted of turnout and some light jog miles without speed training. Less than a week into his vacation, Shorty became bored. He took to digging monstrous holes in his stall every night, which I, the groom, was responsible for filling. We had moved to Orlando, Florida, for the winter season, so it was not unusual for him to dig all the way down to the water line. More than once I arrived at the barn before six A.M. to find him happily splashing around in his own mud hole. Thankfully, his tunneling instincts were curtailed as soon as he started back into full training.

Shorty was a delightful little horse. He approached each day with interest, good humor, and fine effort. I have met only a handful of human beings in my life that I could honestly say the same things about.

CONCLUSIONS

Shorty was a peach of a horse. His personality and training program were more suited for his purpose than was his conformation, but he overcame the last because of the first. He was uncomplicated and fun to deal with and would probably have been good at many other equine endeavors had he the opportunity and training to try them.

CHAPTER EIGHT

THE FEARFUL MIX

THE FEARFUL-MIX HORSE remains basically a fearful-type horse. Under certain circumstances, however, he may display behaviors from another personality type, therefore identifying himself as a mixed personality. In contrast, a purely fearful horse might be passive or aggressive but would not display discernible behaviors from another personality type. The possible combination types are fearful-social, fearful-aloof, and fearful-challenging.

The Fearful-Social Mix

The fearful-social horse may be a little harder to define than some of the other mixes because many fearful horses (especially the passive ones) act in a somewhat social manner once they are comfortable in their environment. The difference between a strictly fearful horse and a fearful-social horse is that the latter is likely to have a somewhat broader comfort range than a horse with only fearful tendencies. In other words, his fearfulness may not be as deep or layered, making him seem less flighty or reactive than a horse of a solely fearful nature.

It is important to remember that even if your horse is fearful-social, and displays many social tendencies, he is still basically a fearful horse and should be handled accordingly.

CASE STUDY: *Van der Amme*

passively fearful

| PASSIVE | 1 | 2 | 3 | 4 | 5 | 6 | 7 | 8 | 9 | 10 | AGGRESSIVE |

passively social

KYB Dressage (Kim and Yvonne Barteau and Company) was invited to Equine Affaire in Massachusetts to present a dressage production number in the nighttime extravaganza the Pfizer Fantasia. The act, a Broadway Quadrille routine, was designed to feature five horses — four Friesians and, in the featured spot, the Grand Prix Dutch Warmblood stallion Liberty, trained by my husband and ridden by my daughter Kassie. We had great music, costuming, and props and just one problem. We had only three Friesians and we needed a fourth.

Enter Van der Amme. This stallion had been imported from Germany as a three-year-old prospect by Max Ots of Ots Sunrise Farms. Like most Friesians, he was beautiful, but he had the added benefits of very good conformation and excellent gaits for dressage. At age four he and another young prospect traveled to Proud Meadows Farm in Texas to be inspected and approved by the German Friesian Society as breeding stallions of very high quality. It was during this stallion inspection that the difficulties began.

Van der Amme was not a typical easy-going, social Friesian, although he acted as if he wished he had more confidence than he currently possessed. He had a passively fearful personality (a 3 or 4 on the aggressivity scale) with a secondary social side. Not only did he lack the typical Friesian composure and confidence, but in addition he had not had enough training time. Consequently, he was judged to be too worried and immature to pass the driving test. His owner was told to put some more training miles on him and then present him at a later date for reinspection. Max, however, decided not to go that route. Since he already had three approved stallions he gelded young Van der Amme and offered him for sale.

Back on the farm in Green Bay, Wisconsin, the gelding, now five years old, was just hanging around with no agenda or regular work program to speak of, still having received little training. Max had kept him on the back burner hoping someone might call or stop by, looking for a horse just like him. When we needed another Friesian for our Quadrille, I asked Max's son Endel (whom Kim and I had employed as a working student for almost two years) about Van der Amme.

Endel called his dad to see if we could borrow Van der Amme for the performance. Max said we were welcome to give him a try, but he made it clear that the horse was a little bit different than the other Friesians they had sent us: he was insecure about new things, and he still had not received any much-needed training.

When Van der Amme did show up, he was a welcome surprise. He had some fearful tendencies, but he was fairly passive about them. He reminded me of the Cowardly Lion in *The Wizard of Oz*, who is embarrassed because he is afraid and deeply wants to have more courage. Although Van der Amme headed into each ride with as much composure as he could muster, new things had a tendency to rattle him. Rather than acting out on this, though, he internalized his fear, holding his breath and tightening the muscles on his topline. He needed miles of work and exposure to new environments, and thus far he had received very little of either.

Despite all of this, you couldn't help but like him. A fine and affable fellow, he kept allowing himself to be reassured, no matter how scared he got. I chose to ride Van der Amme in the drill myself because in general I enjoy working with fearful horses, and in particular I liked everything about this new prospect.

The five-year-old gelding learned a lot of dressage in a very short time. Everything was new to him. He wasn't a lazy horse, and he tried hard to keep his cool. He was similar to many other passively fearful types I had dealt with in the past in that he seemed grateful for the chance to practice his new skills and gain needed poise and assurance. He underwent less than four weeks of practice and training before it was time to head down the road for the three-night performance.

Van der Amme acted like a hillbilly who had scored a ticket to the opera: excited, scared, and unsure how to behave in these new circumstances. Our sole rehearsal went as well as could be expected, with the gelding trying desperately not to be overwhelmed by the busy environment and lose what little composure he possessed. Luckily, the other horses were confident and secure in their work, and consequently Van der Amme gained some much needed buoyancy from them.

The first night was the hardest. The music was loud; the audience even louder. Van der Amme's biggest challenge, however, was the lighting that showcased our act. It is difficult for any rookie horse, much less a fearful type, to figure out what a spotlight is.

It is even harder to believe that the bright circle of light sliding toward him across the dark arena floor will not attack him and cause a grievous injury. Not until Van der Amme stared transfixed at that light making its way determinedly toward him did I realize how hard he was trying not to panic. He seemed fairly certain he might die out there under the lights, but as he stood trembling in the arena, looking at the other horses for guidance and allowing me to reassure him, he gained years' worth of security and self-esteem.

He seemed fairly certain he might die out there under the lights, but as he stood trembling in the arena, looking at the other horses for guidance and allowing me to reassure him, he gained years' worth of security and self-esteem.

When the scary spotlight did not actually kill him, and he emerged unscathed on the other side of the routine, he was almost embarrassingly relieved and pleased with himself. If horses communicate on some tangible level with each other (and I believe they do), then Van der Amme was bragging to the others all through the night about how he had stared down that spotlight. Each night of the performance Van der Amme gained both composure and confidence. By the last night it would be hard for even an educated audience member to pick the fearful horse out of our group.

Thankfully, Van der Amme is still in our barn. A client of ours purchased him, an amateur rider who wanted a Friesian dressage horse. Because she is a little bit timid herself I will introduce Van der Amme to the competition ring when show season starts, before she has to ride him through a test on her own.

I am confident Van der Amme will rise to the occasion. He is a wonderful horse who gains confidence with each new life experience, and I look forward to being part of his future.

CONCLUSIONS

When we first met Van Der Amme, he was a 2 or 3 on the aggressivity scale in terms of his fearful personality. When he was still a stallion and before he had received any training, he was probably a 4 or 5, which, coupled with his lack of training and exposure, would have made him quite a worried individual. I classified him as a fearful-social horse based on the following clues, all of which are more social in origin:

1) Unlike many fearful types, he clearly wanted to be reassured, and his fear did not have as much depth as that of a horse of a strictly fearful character.

2) He was happy and downright interested in the people that surrounded him every day.

3) When he did get overwhelmed, he wanted interaction and was dependent on his handler or rider to fix the problem and help him get comfortable again.

The Fearful-Aloof Mix

The fearful-aloof horse can be tricky to deal with, especially if he is high on the aggressivity scale in expressing his characteristics. A passively fearful-aloof horse will not be nearly as difficult, especially if he has been handled correctly in the past.

A horse with strictly fearful characteristics usually has a better capacity than a fearful-aloof individual for bonding or interacting with his trainer, handler, or owner, which leads to a more interactive relationship in general. A fearful-aloof horse may be reserved and detached even after he has become accustomed to his environment or training situation. Therefore this type is more difficult to develop a working relationship with than many of the other types. I will use an extreme example to help clarify.

CASE STUDY: *Amaretto*

aggressively fearful

PASSIVE | 1 2 3 4 5 6 7 8 9 10 | AGGRESSIVE

aggressively aloof

One of our clients sent us a five-year-old Akhal-Teke stallion that needed some remedial training. He was a beautiful young stallion, a shiny chocolate brown with a finely sculpted face and neck and a nimble, athletic way of moving. Unfortunately, he was also about a 9 on the aggressivity scale in terms of both his fearful and his aloof tendencies. He was prone to random panic attacks, when he would bolt or buck in a quite athletic fashion, and consequently had unseated a lot of fairly experienced riders.

Even in the stall he was a bit of a mess. A weaver, he would sway back and forth with an absent look on his face and then startle violently when you tried to get his attention. He was guarded, panicky, and claustrophobic about what he considered his personal space, and quick and overreactive to many simple requests. It was clear that we had a time-consuming project on our hands.

I have been unseated enough times to proceed with caution when a horse retracts and tightens his back.

The first session with Amaretto started with some longeing to get rid of excess energy. When I climbed on to make the riding assessment, he had that tight, withdrawn, cold-backed feeling that I am always a little cautious about. I have been unseated enough times, right after sensing this, to proceed with caution every time a horse retracts and tightens his back when I first climb aboard.

Amaretto was very sensitive, with hair-trigger reactions to the barest bits of information. He mistrusted any kind of connection, and his lack of confidence in the riding process made it hard to feel settled on his back. A few times he clamped his tail and tried to scoot out from under me. Because he was so reactive, he was also behind the leg and rein aids, having effectively trained his previous riders to be almost too light and sensitive with him. Although he certainly needed all the connection aids, he was so prone to overreacting that it was physically difficult to keep them in place.

After I rode Amaretto for about twenty minutes, he was a little better about all of these issues. I say "a little," because if each little bit of progress were a page in a book, then we had turned the first one, with 299 still to go. Don't get me wrong — all progress, however slight, is beneficial, but in a training perspective this was clearly just the beginning of a long road toward productivity.

At that time in my life I was already a very busy horse trainer with many time constraints. The big test for Amaretto would come when we introduced him to new riders, because he was too time-consuming a project and I had too many projects going to be his only rider. My sixteen-year-old daughter Kassie, who has a very good seat, light hands, and wonderful balance, enjoyed some measure of success with him, but the young stallion was still very inconsistent.

Amaretto bolted on her one morning while both Kim and I were teaching separate lessons in the big indoor arena at Indian Hills. He exploded in the back arena, ran blindly through the main one, and almost jumped into the viewing lounge. Kassie stayed on and he repeated the trip through the back and then the front arena again. He was bolting in the truest sense, running in a blind panic, oblivious to his circumstances or the attempts of his rider to control him. All the time he was gaining momentum, scaring himself further and tuning out Kassie's efforts to steer or stop him. She finally had to bail off, at our insistence because we could not see her recovering the situation.

Kassie was unharmed and we resumed work with Amaretto in the round pen, where he continued to make tentative progress. By now our show season had gotten underway and I informed the owner that this prospect would not make significant progress given our time restrictions. I cautioned him that Amaretto might be very difficult and time-consuming to train and would make progress only in the hands of the right trainer. Gelding him would probably take the edge off some of his tendencies (by moving him down the aggressivity scale); however, it would not change his basic personality, only soften it slightly. We sent him home along with the advice that if Amaretto was going to remain a stallion, his owner should carefully consider the personality type of any mare to whom he might be bred.

CONCLUSIONS

Amaretto is an extreme example of a fearful-aloof horse because he was so high on the aggressivity scale in expressing both of his personality types. Furthermore, because he was very nimble and athletic, quick of both mind and foot, it was much too easy for him to jump out from under his rider whenever he felt he was in a stressful situation. I have worked with other fearful-aloof types that were much easier to handle, control, and relate to, because they were less aggressive about their personality traits and not so high-strung and athletic. The best strategy for this type is as follows:

▶ Begin early, when the horse is young.

▶ Allow plenty of time and patience.

▶ Have a relaxed agenda.

Note: This particular mix, prone to fearful and then disconnected reactions, needs careful handling by a skilled horseman.

The Fearful-Challenging Mix

Unless he is very passive in expressing his personality traits, the fearful-challenging horse can be tricky to train. Most fearful horses are strictly defensive in their reactions when worried or threatened. This mix, however, can turn from defensive to offensive in a hurry. Any horse of this type that is more than a 4 on the aggressivity scale is best handled by a competent and knowledgeable horseman.

CASE STUDY: *That Mustang Mare*

aggressively fearful

PASSIVE 1 2 3 4 5 6 7 8 9 10 AGGRESSIVE

aggressively challenging

I have known only a few horses of this personality mix, but a certain Mustang mare stands out as an aggressive and extremely difficult example.

My friend Sally wandered down to my place in Florida one day and asked if I would go with her to Michigan to collect an unbroken, adopted, ten-year-old Mustang mare that she intended to start under saddle for the owners. This was no small trip, so in exchange she offered to let me half-fill her stock trailer with good Michigan hay (which is a lot better than Florida hay) and bring it home for my horses.

Since her adoption the previous year the mare had produced a filly, who at ten months was still not weaned. Part of our mission, therefore, was to separate her from that baby so each could develop their own relationship with the owners.

When we arrived at the modest Michigan farm it was already dark. Sally wanted to see the mare right away. The pair were housed in a 20-square-foot stall that opened directly into a big turnout with 6-foot-high solid panel fencing. The mare and baby were locked in at night but could go in or out at will during the day. The mare was a homely, scruffy bay with a long face and a wild eye, and the baby was so muddy I couldn't tell what color she might be.

Trembling and twitching, ears back, the mare

watched Sally approach.

Neither creature had ever had a human hand on her, but that did not faze Sally. When she entered the stall, the mare instantly moved in front of her foal. Trembling and twitching, ears back, the horse looked both scared and mad as she watched Sally approach. If it had been me in that stall I would not have kept walking toward the mare, but Sally and I were not cut from the same piece of cloth. She continued to inch toward the pair, talking soothingly, her hand outstretched.

The mare, her rump facing her intruder, waited quietly until the woman was almost at her flank, then took a step backward and let her have it: a double-barrel kick with both hind legs that caught Sally in the thighs and sent her flying through the air. The mare then crowded her baby into the corner and resumed her stance.

I helped Sally up. She could barely walk, but nothing was broken. When we went up to the house I asked if she wanted to abandon the whole deal. She refused to quit while that mare had one up on her. Horse people can be so stubborn.

The next morning Sally was barely mobile. I rigged up a chute so we could herd the mare into our stock trailer and shut the young one in the stall. The mare was both crazy-scared and crazy-mean, and it took almost an hour to separate her and her baby. When we finally closed the door on the mare, she lit into the inside of the trailer like a bucking bronco. She dented that thing up in less than five minutes.

I again asked Sally if she wanted to bail, but her sense of humor had returned. Heck, she said, the hard part is over. Now we just have to get her broke.

We. I had my doubts.

Once at Sally's place we backed the trailer right up to a stall to unload the mare. I suggested that Sally invite one of the teenage boys who always hung out at the feed store to be the first to climb aboard the horse. I myself did not want the honor of mounting such an unlikely prospect for the first time. After warning her again to be careful, I took my hay and headed home.

I heard nothing for a week, and then Sally stopped by to tell me that the "hell mare" had barged past her when she opened the stall, cleared a 5-foot fence with ease, and disappeared onto her neighbors' 300-acre cow ranch. Would I get one of my horses and help fetch her? Of course, except we didn't succeed in fetching her that day, nor the next, nor the next after that. It was more than a week before we got the mare back on to Sally's property. Although she still had not admitted it, I knew Sally was finally thinking this mare was far more trouble than she was worth.

A couple of days later the teenage boys at the feed store had their own stories. Turns out three or four of them had gotten flying lessons from Sally's training project. No one was hurt, but that wily mare had earned a begrudging respect from the lot. While none wanted to admit fear, they were all complaining and dragging their heels at the thought of Round 2 on Saturday.

The mare's circumstances, her long feral history, her challenging personality, and her owners' inexperience made it hard for me to visualize her ever being reliable about anything except being dangerous and unpredictable. Although she had reluctantly accepted her current situation she was neither settled nor content. She seemed to be biding her time and waiting for an opportunity to either throw down or run off. I felt that no matter who handled her she would be a difficult and dodgy prospect.

I accompanied Sally on her return trip to Michigan. Although the owners were thrilled at their wild adoptee's slight improvement, the mare lost little time basking in their good humor. She unseated the lady within thirty seconds of mounting and scared her good. We suggested that they leave the mare alone and see if the baby turned out any better.

Driving home with another load of hay, Sally and I agreed that the horse was one in a million, but not in a good way. We had both been involved with other adopted Mustangs, none of whom was nearly as difficult as this mare and many of whom had become reliable riding horses. In fact, I may go out on a limb and say that if I had ten horses just like that mare to break and train, I might have switched careers and investigated becoming a librarian or an astronaut.

The good news is that among the hundreds of equine subjects that I have worked with over the last few decades, this mare's position at the bottom of the list of horses I would agree to work with is still very secure.

CONCLUSIONS

The mare was an extreme example of this personality mix, being very aggressive (about a 9) in expressing both her fearful and her challenging traits. Her unique history and environmental circumstances contributed greatly to her unsuitability as a riding and training project:

▶ Being born and living in the wild;

▶ Being adopted by inexperienced owners;

▶ Not being handled by humans even after her adoption;

▶ Having an unweaned foal of whom she was so protective.

Any horse of this personality type that is higher than a 6 or 7 on the aggressivity scale needs to be handled with a great deal of respect by a knowledgeable horseman.

CHAPTER NINE

THE ALOOF MIX

THE DIFFERENCE BETWEEN a strictly aloof horse and a mix is that the former, no matter what kind of trouble or conflict he gets into, will only slide up and down the aggressivity scale of his own personality type. An aloof mix, in contrast, occasionally borrows behaviors from another type. Aloof-social, aloof-fearful, and aloof-challenging are the possible mixes for an aloof horse.

The Aloof-Social Mix

Of all the horse personalities, this is one of the easiest to deal with (especially those individuals on the passive end of the scale). This personality is often confused with the strictly aloof type. In fact, many aloof horses that are described by their owners as having social-type behavior are actually aloof horses that have caught on to some sort of snack program.

When we have an aloof horse in the barn, I tell the kids who work for me that they need to encourage the horse to react and respond to them often. This is best done (and sometimes can only be done) with treats and with extra attention at grooming time. Any horse that gets enough treats and likes them is going to start looking for them. That does not mean he is turning into a social horse; it just means your training strategy toward improved interaction is working.

The aloof-social horse will not have such deeply aloof tendencies as his strictly aloof counterpart will. He is also more interactive in a herd situation than aloof horses with no social characteristics. An aloof-social individual will give you the impression that there is a friendly horse hiding behind a rather reserved exterior.

CASE STUDY: *Zayere*

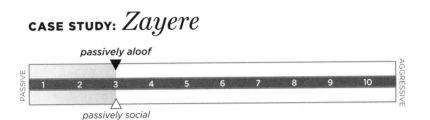

passively aloof

passively social

Although I knew Zayere for only a few days, I will remember him forever. A white-gray Arabian stallion, he was less than 15 hands high and about ten or twelve years old when I met him. I won't forget him because he was my equine partner for the Tevis Cup.

For anyone unfamiliar with the world of endurance racing, the Tevis Cup is one of the toughest and most challenging 100-mile races in the country. I had the privilege of being Zayere's ignorant passenger on this remarkable journey.

When, you might ask, did I become an endurance rider? Good question: I did not, but when I was invited to ride the race, I said: "Sounds like fun." I figured that 100 miles couldn't be too hard, since I ride horses all day, every day. I'd just keep riding the same one. It sounded like a great life experience.

The Tevis starts at a camp outside Truckee, California, and ends less than 24 hours later in Auburn, beginning at an elevation of about 7,000 feet and descending to about 1,500 feet by the finish. But unless you are familiar with the terrain in that part of the country, however, those facts will tell you nothing. I won't give you a Tevis tutorial, but if you are interested there is plenty of information available about both the race and the terrain (see References).

This story is about Zayere, whom I met at the finish line of the race, traveled with to the start, and then rode for one day. Zayere was an aloof-social horse and fairly passive about both of these traits considering that he was a stallion. A businesslike little fellow, he accepted me into our partnership with mild indifference. Foolishly, I was excited about this big adventure, not truly grasping the magnitude or difficulty of the endeavor. Looking back, I can only compare myself to someone showing up for the United States Grand Prix Dressage Championships to compete on a borrowed horse after just a handful of dressage lessons.

The Tevis Cup is serious business, with serious riders who have trained themselves and their horses for months, if not years, before entering. I had shown up on a lark, in response to a challenge thrown out by Bob, the owner of the farm in Illinois where we trained dressage horses. He and his brother Jim, an experienced and accomplished endurance rider, had ridden in the Tevis together on a previous occasion. In addition, the brothers had recently competed together in the Ironman Triathlon in Hawaii, which meant their general fitness level was far greater than mine. Brother Jim kept a few endurance horses in training at his farm in Montana and that is where Zayere had come from.

I did not consciously analyze the stallion's personality when I met him, but when you have studied horses for a while, individual personalities come at you anyway, along with observations about their conformation and rideability. Zayere seemed somewhat removed or unreachable, as if he would wait to see if I passed muster before making a judgment call. I had one practice ride on him: we rode out and back from the finish line before trailering up to Truckee. Under saddle, Zayere was a capable little horse, businesslike and confident about his work. It was apparent that someone had trained him well. He knew his job, knew why we were there, and made it clear that he would require little help from me.

He knew his job, knew why we were there,

and made it clear that he would require little help from me.

Endurance racing is unlike any other equine sport I had participated in. There is no elaborate grooming or tacking ceremony, no blue shampoo, no braiding of mane and tail, no dress code or uniform for the rider. The horses are not pampered or babied; nor do they work only on groomed, pristine footing or sleep on mounds of shavings every night. Quite the contrary. Endurance horses are fit, tough horses with fit, educated riders who are willing to pit themselves against both the clock and the rugged course. By the time we mounted up at 4:30 in the morning on the dusty little logging trail we would start on, I was realizing that poor Zayere was likely the most handicapped horse there.

And there were a lot of horses. Approximately 240 mounts and riders were milling around the start before embarking down that dry, narrow path. Instantly, my eyes and contact lenses filled with dirt. I started right at that moment to make a list in my head of all the things I should have known about or brought with me. Number one was to have at least read a book on endurance racing before jumping in at the top. Number two would be a set of those goggles that everyone else had on. Numbers three on (I lost count) ranged from proper footwear, information about tailing, and what the many vet checks consisted of, to at least knowing who the good riders were. You name it, I didn't know it.

The Tevis Cup is about hard riding, rough terrain, and vet checks. Every 20 miles or so (more often during the more strenuous portions of the course), there are stringent vet checks where the horses are meticulously examined to avoid injuries due to overexertion. Zayere, oblivious to my ignorance about endurance racing, skated through his first three or four checks with ease.

By the 50-mile marker I had lost both Bob and brother Jim to the perils of the course. Jim had been pulled at the 32-mile mark by one of the vets, and Bob dove off Fred (his Anglo-Arab gelding and a prior Tevis cup winner) into the American River when we crossed it, promising to catch up with me later down the trail. I next saw him waving at me from the cab of a truck carrying himself and Fred to the 72-mile marker.

During the entire ride Zayere behaved like a prince. He seemed to need nothing from me, and when we met other horses on the trail he would ignore them until they parted company with us. Then he would whinny a little goodbye or make a half-hearted effort to stay with them even if they were not traveling at our pace. Soon after we broke contact with them, he would return to his businesslike way of heading down the trail, seeming to know much more clearly than I just where the finish line might be.

By this point it was dark, and I realized that those glowsticks I had forgotten to put in my saddlebag would have been handy right about now to light the desperately dark and somewhat treacherous path. I couldn't see a thing. I wondered if bears or mountain lions ever jumped on dumb endurance riders who had lost their way.

The last big vet check was after the 87th mile. We arrived there at about 10:30 P.M. to find that fewer than thirty horses out of the original 200-plus had made it that far. I knew we had lots of time, and instead of running Zayere through the vet check while he was still warm and limber, I chose to let him have a rest and eat some bran mash.

I presented him near the end of my time allotment. When I trotted him out for the vets' inspection, one of them (whom we had seen at the first checkpoint, and who had questioned my inclusion into the race at all) said the horse looked a little stiff and would need to be pulled from the competition. The second vet did not really see it, but after jogging again Zayere was declared out and I had to walk him two miles down to a trailer that would take us back to the finish.

I felt bad for Zayere. I was sure he knew what had happened. He had been surer of himself than I was the entire day. I imagine any veteran endurance horse knows that you don't finish the race in a trailer, and I know my ignorance was the only thing that kept him from finishing. Zayere deserved to finish. If he carried my unhelpful self that far, imagine what he would have done with a real endurance rider.

At any rate, he was not injured and the next day came out of his stall in great shape and with good humor intact. Physically and mentally he was none the worse for wear. The Tevis Cup was a fun experience for me (unfortunately at the risk of Zayere's success), and I learned a lot from the experience.

CONCLUSIONS

I have known quite a few aloof-social horses in my time, but Zayere is the most fun to remember because I can connect him to such a unique life experience. Here are four of his indicators:

1) Zayere exhibited steady good humor yet was self-sufficient.

2) Although he showed little need for interaction, he did not shun it.

3) He understood his work and was businesslike and focused.

4) His personality traits were subtle and almost invisible, typical of an aloof horse.

He was fairly passive in expressing all of his characteristics (at most a 3), and if he hadn't been a stallion his personality might have been all but invisible. He was a reserved but affable fellow and probably would have made a suitable mount for almost any rider in almost any venue.

It is interesting to note that passively aloof stallions are usually very "non-stallionlike" in their behavior, acting almost like geldings instead.

The Aloof-Fearful Mix

The aloof-fearful horse is a reserved but watchful character. The aloof horse's indifference to small actions or requests is in stark contrast to a fearful type's sensitive or overreactive behavior. This type will have the most success when handled and ridden by a clearheaded, methodical, and empathetic rider.

CASE STUDY: *Pahan*

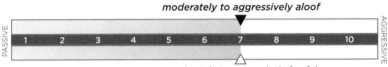

moderately to aggressively aloof

PASSIVE 1 2 3 4 5 6 7 8 9 10 AGGRESSIVE

moderately to aggressively fearful

I met Pahan, a twelve-year-old Akhal-Teke stallion from Russia, when he came in for some remedial training a few years ago. Akhal-Tekes are narrow, intelligent, and light-boned horses, reputed to have a very high endurance level. I had not witnessed their rather flat, aerodynamic way of moving in any other breed and I found them fascinating.

Pahan had been a riding horse for years, first in Russia and then at a few different locations in the United States. He presented an immediate challenge for our program: first, because I was not familiar with the breed; and second, because he was an absolute mess under saddle. Although fit and athletic, he was alternately confused and worried by the whole training idea.

In fact, this twitchy black stallion had more training issues and backward ideas than any horse I had ever met. Having almost made an art form out of being behind the leg (the dressage term

Pahan at Grand Prix 2005.

for not freely moving forward from light leg pressure), he was so stiff and tight from not going forward that he could barely move. He was also very defensive in the bridle and had retreated both physically and mentally from all of the aids.

Pahan was easy to identify as an aloof-fearful horse on our first meeting. He tuned out the riding aids until he felt he might get into trouble, and then he would either run backward until he hit the arena wall or jolt forward and try to run away while keeping his neck, poll, and jaw locked. He ignored the leg aids and then kicked defensively at them if you used stronger ones. I did not sense that he was angry or challenging, just desperately defensive.

Once we developed a connection that worked, Pahan began to make rapid progress up the dressage ladder. He proved to be one of the most intelligent horses I have ever worked with, and as soon

WORKING WITH PAHAN

Pahan was a funny little horse. His nature told him to ignore and retreat from the aids, but when pressured to pay attention, he displayed over-reactionary fearful and panicky behaviors. It took a few days of riding just to start to develop a working relationship under saddle.

Since aloof horses do not pay enough attention anyway, I needed to clear up the action-reaction, one aid-one answer part of the equation (see page 188) and make sure he understood what the aids meant. I went back to basics in a snaffle and worked on going to the bit and lots of suppling exercises. He responded almost gratefully to this new program of easy-to-understand questions and straightforward, uncomplicated answers.

as he developed a workable learning ethic, he absorbed and made good use of all the information he received during training.

He has matured into a fun horse both to ride and to train. Although still somewhat removed and guarded by nature, he likes to work and understands our training program. He is certainly not lazy, and he is extremely clever. In the more than two years that he has been with us, he has gone from below 50 percent at Training Level to a 65 percent at the Grand Prix. (See glossary.)

Now a gelding, Pahan is as comfortable in his work as I can expect such a reserved yet fearful horse to be. His unique appearance and movement make him a wonderful ambassador for the breed. He is now ready to start his second season at the Grand Prix, and I plan on making him my next bridle-less exhibition horse so he can have something new to work on.

CONCLUSIONS

Here are four clues that helped me identify Pahan initially as an aloof-fearful combination:

1) He would ignore the aids for as long as possible and then react explosively.

2) Alternatively, he would totally ignore the aids one second and then overreact to them the next.

3) He would often be dramatically defensive.

4) He might have a fit of panic for no apparent reason.

When I met Pahan he was about a 7 on the aggressivity scale in terms of his aloof tendencies. His fearful character ranged from about a 6 to an 8 whenever he displayed it. After he was gelded and in a more cohesive training program, he settled down to a consistent 4 or 5 in terms of both of his personality types.

CASE STUDY: *Eloise*

Eloise was born at Indian Hills the year before we moved there from Florida. When we met her she was an unweaned chestnut yearling running frantically behind her aggressively fearful mother on about 200 acres of pasture. The filly's sire, Limmerick (see page 190), was an aggressively social Dutch Warmblood.

Neither Eloise nor her mother had been handled at all since the foal's birth, and consequently she was like a little wild animal when we corralled her and her mother and brought them to the barn. I won't delve into the details of the halter-breaking and weaning ceremony, but it was a long one requiring a good deal of patience and skill. We were more interested in the filly than we were in her mother, so after worming, shots, and some basic handling, we turned the mare back out with the herd to deal with at a later time.

Eloise was beautiful, athletic, panicky, claustrophobic, and disassociative. She was nearly frenzied in her stall, so we had to keep watch over her for the first day and a half in case she tried to throw herself into the barn aisle. Although she did launch herself at the door a few times, she never made it over, and eventually she quit trying to escape.

The settling process took days. We were patient, and rather than worry her needlessly with too many strangers, we assigned just one of our working students for all of the filly's initial bonding and handling. Because Eloise needed the handling and socialization, Kim and I decided to keep her in the barn, with daily turnout, for a year before her first backing. Although she was tricky to catch both in her stall and in her turnout, Nancy (her groom) enjoyed more success getting a hand on her than the rest of us did.

Because she had such a strong mixture of both aloof and fearful characteristics, Eloise remained difficult to deal with. She seemed to live in her own world, and when you finally captured her attention she would overreact or panic about something she had just recently been observed to ignore. Her reactions were sporadic and often explosive and it took much handling, patience, and time to get through to her.

When it came time to start her under saddle, Nancy was there with her every day. Because almost everything worried the filly, and she was prone to hair-trigger reactions, we proceeded slowly and took the time to introduce each new piece of equipment gradually. At times it appeared that she did not want us to interact with her. She would retreat to the corner of her stall, put her butt to the door, and tune out everything. We were careful never to take her comfort level for granted and to slow down and reassure her as often as was necessary. When we did finally back her, she managed to get out from under three of us, including her friend Nancy. It was not ill-intended: she was just very disassociative, quick, and athletic. She startled randomly for no observable reasons, and it was tough to stay with her.

Over the course of a year Eloise became a lovely riding mount, responding best to a fair but quiet rider, but comfortable only in one-on-one relationships. Eventually she was sold and we lost track of her. Although she was a wonderfully talented mare, she had a hard time gaining comfort in our world because of her own aggressively aloof and fearful personality traits and the primary influence during her first year of her aggressively fearful mother.

To avoid repeating such a scenario, the owner could breed Eloise's dam to a more passive stallion. The mare should then foal indoors so the filly can be imprinted and socialized from birth.

CONCLUSIONS

Eloise was like a feral horse when we first met her. Other young horses in the herd with her shared similar environmental circumstances, but because of her aggressive personality traits she was the most difficult to get through to. Here are three obvious signals:

1) She was dangerous to catch and load into a stock trailer even when she was with her mother, and our biggest fear was that she would hurt herself (as aggressively fearful and aggressively aloof horses can be prone to doing).

2) She was also quite wild during the weaning process, and again we feared she would injure herself (which she did experiment with by trying to dive into the barn aisle).

3) Finally she bonded reasonably well with one person who was a low-key individual herself (a suitable type for such a horse) and eventually we made progress with her.

She was more difficult to handle than many other horses because she had an aggressive mix of two personality types. With the worst kind of beginning that a horse of her personality extremes could have, she consequently was an 8 or 9 on the aggressivity scale, in terms of both her fearful and aloof characteristics, when we first met her. By the time she was sold, she was down to a 5 or 6, with her fearful tendencies taking a back seat to her more clearly defined aloof character. Had she been born in a barn and handled since birth, she would have had a much easier time with her starting process.

The Aloof-Challenging Mix

The aloof-challenging horse differs from a strictly aloof horse by borrowing behaviors from the challenging personality during certain situations. While horses of this character may act reserved or detached most of the time, certain stimuli (such as the various interactions in a herd or training situation) may cause them to act in a threatening, territorial, or challenging manner. Depending on where such horses fit on the aggressivity scale, behavior can range from reserved and a little testy to very removed and then threatening.

Note: I must reiterate that even when this or any type reverts to argumentative or challenging actions, it is essential to deal with the horse's behavior and not "get into the argument."

CASE STUDY: *Nicki*

moderately aloof

PASSIVE	1	2	3	4	5	6	7	8	9	10	AGGRESSIVE

moderately to aggressively challenging

Nicki deliberately broke my ankle. This happened because her personality and her prior training led her to behave in a way that made injuries a very real threat for anyone who rode her. A plain brown Morgan mare, seven years old when we met, she came to me in my "desperate horse trainer will train anything for money" days in Eustis, Florida. Self-confident, with a high opinion of herself, she had a moderately to aggressively aloof personality with some moderately to aggressively challenging tendencies right behind it.

Nicki had been carefully cultivating a dangerous rearing problem. She did not rear because she was scared, nor because she was confused. She reared because it scared people and made them get off her and leave her alone.

Her first instinct told her to ignore the aids, but if her previous trainers or adult amateur owner insisted, she challenged the request and reared repeatedly until they gave up and got off. The request that set her off could be as simple as "one more circle," "please flex right," or "walk away from the barn."

As a rule, rearing is something amateur riders should not mess with. It is a habit that's dangerous for both horse and rider and needs to be remedied by a professional. I guess I wasn't quite professional enough in those early days, because Nicki certainly got the better of me.

I was riding her in my front field and she was through with listening to me less than five minutes into the ride. When I gave her the reins and kicked her to move her on, she stood up. The footing was a little soft and a little deep, so she lost her balance and flipped over. Although I could tell she was coming over, I could not get one of my feet out of the stirrups, and she broke my ankle when she fell on it.

As a rule, rearing is something amateur riders should

not mess with. It is a habit that's dangerous for both horse

and rider and needs to be remedied by a professional.

I have had plenty of falls in my lifetime, resulting in strains, sprains, bruises, and cracked ribs, but that fall off Nicki hurt a lot. I consider any spill or injury caused by the deliberate bad behavior of a horse to be much more serious than the falling-off incident all riders will encounter if they ride long enough. This fall was not an accident: it was caused by a spoiled, bad-tempered mare determined to have her way.

I had to leave Nicki alone while my son helped me back to the house and then went back out and untacked her for me, but I had no intention of giving up on the problem. Horse people can be ridiculously stubborn about not allowing any equine to get the better of them, and I have never been an exception to that.

Her owner and I discussed our options. Laurel knew that the mare was both unrideable and unsellable while she had this dangerous habit. She did not want to put her down, nor did she want to market her as a broodmare and then have somebody try to ride her for fun and get hurt. I told her I had a few ideas about how to cure the mare, and she gave me permission to carry on with my training.

Within a week I was back to work, with Advil and a homemade walking cast to help me out. I hooked the mare up with a pair of long lines and a surcingle and drove her back to the scene of the crime. I longed her a bit and then started to line her up ahead of me as if we were going to have a driving lesson. I gathered her onto a contact so she could feel the influence of my hands on the long reins establishing the fact that she now had to pay complete attention to me.

Less than a minute later she was on her hind legs. She actually twisted in mid-air and came threateningly toward me. I did what any self-respecting broken-footed horse trainer would do: I sidestepped her and then helped her fall on her side with the long reins. She got up, reared, and charged me again. She fell down again. The third time she hit the ground she had the wind knocked out of her. She got up slowly and humbly and looked at me out of the corner of her eye. It was clear that she was through misbehaving for the day.

In fact, she was through for good. Nicki never reared again. She was smart and athletic, so training proceeded relatively smoothly from then on. I taught her to pull a cart while my foot was healing and then went back to riding her.

She ended up being one heck of a horse and I liked her a lot. I did some basic dressage with her, which she tolerated and absorbed, but what she really liked was team penning. Unafraid of the atmosphere, she liked bossing those cows around. She was my Saturday night team-penning partner for quite some time.

While I would not recommend that others try what I had to do with that mare in order to get her to stop rearing, it was worth it in Nicki's case. I was able to cure her bad habit without hurting her, and I gained her respect in the process. Nicki ended up as a reliable, useful, and productive horse, eventually owned by a teenage girl who had great fun with her.

CONCLUSIONS

Nicki was about a 6 on the aggressivity scale in terms of her aloof tendencies when I met her. Her challenging characteristics were closer to a 7 because she had become so spoiled and intent on having her own way.

Here were three clues for identifying her particular mix:

1) She would ignore and then challenge the aids.

2) She was self-sufficient.

3) To achieve her goal of being left alone she developed the dangerous habit of rearing.

After about a year of training, it would be hard to notice any challenging behavior from her at all. She was smart enough to know what she could get away with, and once respect and a learning attitude were achieved she made readable, reliable progress.

CASE STUDY: *Angelo*

moderately to aggressively aloof

PASSIVE | 1 | 2 | 3 | 4 | 5 | 6 | 7 | 8 | 9 | 10 | AGGRESSIVE

passively challenging

In life, it's said, you learn more from your failures than from your successes. Angelo was both a very difficult and a very humbling horse for me, and I did indeed learn a great deal from him. He wasn't exactly a failure, therefore, but he was a blow to my ego. I suppose everyone needs that from time to time.

My husband Kim and I met Angelo by way of a videotape that a colleague had brought over from Germany. The thirteen-year-old dark bay gelding, videotaped at a German sale barn, was ridden and presented by a skilled professional Grand Prix rider.

I could clearly see the training issues. Angelo was stiff in the poll and jaw and often not quick enough to answer the many leg aids an FEI-level horse must immediately respond to. I could also tell, even from the videotape, that he had some obvious aloof tendencies. He appeared slow in responding to his rider's aids, and although the riding arena was crowded, he made no effort to interact with any of the comings or goings that surrounded him.

The other thing I could see (and frankly, the only thing I paid enough attention to) was his dynamic and extravagant way of moving. He had expressive and animated movement, big sweeping half-passes and picture-perfect lead changes. He knew all of the FEI movements, and I was convinced that with a little finishing and suppling work he would make an incredible competition horse.

Rather than take the time to go over and look at the horse ourselves, Kim and I made some arrangements and purchased the rangy gelding after some negotiations and a vetting. At that time I was suffering from overconfidence because I had enjoyed some success with other horses that had been deemed difficult or unrideable by my peers. Consequently, I figured that whatever Angelo's issues were, I would be able to set him right in short order. (Humble pie, anyone?)

Our first ride was an eye-opener for me.

Although Angelo did not misbehave in any tangible way,

he had a very deliberate and well-defined habit

of just tolerating the aids without

actually responding to them.

Soon Angelo was in our barn. I was excited to see him in the flesh and couldn't wait for him to settle in so we could begin to build our working relationship. Our first ride, however, was an eye-opener for me. Although Angelo did not misbehave in any tangible way, he had a very deliberate and well-defined habit of just tolerating the aids without actually responding to them. I did not try to fix anything at that time; rather, I gathered information from the horse, had Kim watch him go, and started to devise a training program in my mind.

It was obvious that Angelo had some aggressively aloof tendencies. That's all I could determine about his personality type at that time, since I had been trying not to influence him beyond his comfort zone as yet. (Pushing a horse past his comfort zone is not required in order to make a fair personality evaluation, but it does bring latent matters to the surface.) I had the uneasy feeling that Angelo was used to being muscled around, and I suspected that soft contact and small requests were not part of his working vocabulary. It also seemed likely that the FEI work Angelo had been demonstrating at the sale barn in Germany might not be of the variety that would be accessible in the show ring. That meant I would be much too busy getting my movements to happen than would be appropriate for competition.

So it was back to basics. I put a snaffle bridle on him and tried to work him as if he were a First Level horse, but he would have none of it. If I didn't let him lean on the rein he would raise his head like a giraffe and build momentum with each lap of the arena, refusing to acknowledge either my half-halts or the suppling aids. In fact, he chose to dive into the connection, trying to set his poll and jaw against the bridle while he lined himself up crookedly behind it, drifting off to the right at every opportunity. I let him keep his head up and continued to ride forward toward a connection that never did materialize. I then realized that while he was not lazy (he was content to move forward at my request), he was never really ahead of my leg. That is where the next problem came to light.

The next day I took him out for some hand-galloping in the farm's five-acre berm. I hoped that once he got rolling in a bigger arena he might loosen up and start to use his back a little more productively. Angelo did not have the same idea at all. He put his head in the air and refused to gallop at all unless he was allowed to lean on my hands. When I insisted with leg and whip that he must move forward anyway, he quit tuning me out and started to argue. He kicked at my leg, reared, and spun in an effort to get back to the barn, grabbed the bit and leaned on it, and attempted numerous other infractions and evasions that made me realize he was also a little spoiled and maybe a little bit challenging.

When I let go of the reins and kicked him again, he launched into the flat, tight, stiff-backed canter that horses do when they are determined to stay behind your leg. I finally got him to do a couple of laps around the arena without slowing down or leaning on my hands, but he was far from where I needed him to be. I began to wonder how the demonstration rider had managed to ride him so productively on that videotape from Germany. She obviously possessed skills and strategies that surpassed my own.

Progress was desperately slow. Kim continued to bolster me with speeches about how important these basic issues were and how it didn't matter about the time frame when you were correcting training problems. Although I persevered, I felt I was having very little impact because Angelo tuned me out and withdrew mentally from my training program. Unwilling to stay ahead of my leg and not lean on my hand, he was determined to start every day with the same problems we had addressed the day before.

During this initial riding phase I had also been working to foster a more productive overall horse-rider relationship with Angelo. By now he had defined himself to me as an aggressively aloof type with a challenging undertone. He often stood with his head in the corner of the stall, tuning out the barn activities and interacting with no one. I took to bringing him his favorite treat, a banana, once or twice a day, calling to him and waiting until he walked over to the door to get his reward. I doled out his treat in small pieces while I scratched his neck and socialized with him.

Before long the sound of my voice in the barn aisle would bring him forward to his gate with ears up and an expectant look on his face. Although this bait-and-bribe technique appeals mostly to a horse's taste buds and does not address his real training issues, it can be useful for generating positive interactions with a new subject. Whenever possible I groomed Angelo myself, taking time to discover and cater to his preferred routine. I also turned him out in the sand lot so he could roll and scratch his back. While all of these activities served to strengthen our relationship on the ground, I still had not made enough progress under saddle.

By this time show season in Illinois was well underway, and I started to get show-ring fever. Angelo was a talented horse and I wanted a chance to show him off. I went back to the double bridle to see if the snaffle work had improved things, and they had. The big gelding was not cured, but I had made tangible progress. He was still behind my leg, and his responses to the rein aids and the connection in general could be described as stiff, dull, and hanging, but with no speedier alternative I carried on with my program.

I started schooling dressage tests, hoping some sequences might help him get more in tune with the aids. I found that even with his training issues he could do all of the easier FEI work, meaning everything except passage and piaffe, to a reasonable degree. The sad part was that while the work he was doing was passable, Angelo was far from a passable sort of horse. He had the gaits, strength, and presence of a superior dressage star, but I could not seem to "get it together" with him. Occasionally he showed glimpses of incredible movement and talent, but then he would stiffen or tune me out right when I needed him, and the moment of sheer brilliance would seem like a mirage.

Back home I went through all of my books, looking for answers to my dilemma and finding nothing. I started feeling like a doctor who has been entrusted to cure someone of a disease he cannot even diagnose with certainty. I do not easily become discouraged, and every time I started to feel hopeless Angelo would flash at me a brilliant bit of work and the possibility of a partnership. Quick to keep me in my place, he would immediately remind me that I would not be allowed to access his brilliance on my timetable, and my frustration continued.

I finally got impatient enough to take him to some shows where, more often than not, he scored better than he should have. The judges could see his talent, but not all of them could discern the connection issues that still plagued our daily rides. Although we had some really good scores during our first season together, I knew he was not working the way a dressage horse of his caliber should. When show season ended I redoubled my efforts, returning to each basic connection issue and addressing it thoroughly.

By now Angelo looked like a different horse. He was almost fat, with a sleek, dappled, dark bay coat and layers of new muscling on his neck, back, and topline. More interactive in the barn, he now spent more time with his head over the stall door, looking for snacks, than he did in the corner. Sometimes even after consuming his treats he would stay, his head over the door, watching with interest the activity and bustle in the barn aisle. He was content to ride outside now and all traces of spoiled behavior and barn sourness were gone.

I had made progress. I should have been happy, content, and satisfied with my work, but I was not. Angelo was a horse of superior athletic ability and talent. If all that power and extravagant movement was in there, then why couldn't I connect with it?

The answer was in his personality. Angelo didn't want to stay tuned in to me under saddle, and he was hard to connect with because he would zone out when I rewarded him, rather than relaxing and awaiting my next bit of information. Each time he zoned out I had only a 30 to 40 percent chance of getting him back on the aids in time for my next request.

Horses can't learn anything if there is no reward.

So what was the solution? Should I not soften or reward him when he complied, for fear I could not regain his attention? That didn't seem right. Horses can't learn anything if there is no reward, and it doesn't have to be treats: it just has to be something that remains consistent and reliable. If I couldn't soften when he obeyed a rein aid, I would certainly be heading down the wrong road. He seemed almost to want me to bully him, and while this is necessary when a horse is trying to bully you or you are correcting misbehaviors, it is not advisable as a daily training practice and was therefore not an option.

The physical work of the FEI movements was much easier for Angelo than the required mental discipline; many horses that I had worked with were completely the opposite. I had trained and known numerous horses by this time, and none as talented as Angelo, so why had they all made more progress than he?

At this writing Angelo is still with us. Kim graciously decided to jump in and put more miles of basics on him. Kim is a much more methodical and systematic trainer than I am, and this tedious and at times unrewarding routine work does not frustrate him the way that it does me. Angelo has continued to make progress; in fact my daughter Kassie will debut him at Grand Prix this season. Angelo is a case of a super-talented horse who will never reach his full potential. If we had acquired him as a five-year-old, however, I suspect that things would have been different.

CONCLUSIONS

An aloof-challenging type, Angelo registers at an 8 on the aggressivity scale in terms of his aloof characteristics and about a 3 about his challenging ones. He proved to be a difficult subject for these reasons:

- He was thirteen when we brought him over and already fairly set in his ways.

- His basic personality type meant that it would be hard for him to stay attentive enough, often enough, to create better association and response to the aids.

CHAPTER TEN

THE CHALLENGING MIX

The challenging mix remains essentially a challenging horse. However, this mix will borrow behaviors from another personality type on occasion, rather than simply slide up and down the aggressivity scale of his personality. There are three possible mixes for a challenging horse: challenging-social, challenging-fearful, and challenging-aloof.

The Challenging-Social Mix

The challenging-social horse will borrow social-type actions on regular occasions. The horses I've met who classify as challenging-social seem to have more of a sense of humor about life than their strictly challenging counterparts do. They are not quite so aggressive in group turnout or herd situations and readily form equine friendships. They still prefer to be the boss (unless they are out with an even more aggressively challenging type than themselves), but overall they are not quite as determined to have things their way as a horse with strictly challenging characteristics.

Challenging-social types are usually very interactive horses and keep careful track of their handling. It is best when dealing with this type that you do the same.

CASE STUDY: *Hey You Star*

I met an engaging young Arabian mare at the large and prestigious Scottsdale Arabian Horse Show held every February in Arizona. Hey You Star was a four-year-old liver chestnut mare owned at that time by a very well-respected and well-known breeder of Arabian horses.

Ridiculously cute, she had a mischievous face with large, wide-set, intelligent eyes, and amazing facial expressions that gave a pretty clear indication of her mood. She stood about 14.2 hands high and was an energetic and talented mover with a phenomenally uphill and well-balanced canter. Her base personality was passively to moderately challenging, but she had a social side behind it.

When I met her, she was tearing around the warm-up arena at a rather reckless pace, with what appeared to be an overwhelmed and frustrated training apprentice on her back. Hey You's tack consisted of a hunt-seat saddle, a running martingale, and a full cheek snaffle bridle. She was fighting for possession of her head and neck and was clearly winning the battle.

I had been assigned to ride the athletic young mare in some Sport Horse Under Saddle classes at this show, and we had two days to get used to each other. I flagged down the apprentice on board and told her I would like to ride. I removed the martingale, adjusted my stirrups, and climbed on the diminutive young mare.

It is a funny thing about challenging horses: they are always trying to tell you things. This little mare was no exception. She started to dictate to me where she liked to carry her head, how fast she thought she should go, and how much she didn't like leg aids in general. A horse of many opinions, she was determined to share them all, and I have always been partial to horses so willing to interact. However, I was not about to be bossed around by a pint-sized Arabian mare, no matter how cute or opinionated she was.

I let her dash around the arena for a while, although I had no intention of tiring her out. That rarely works anyway, and almost never with an Arabian. Besides, Hey You Star felt like one of those horses who are easier to communicate with when they are moving. Part of the reason she was dashing around was that she didn't like my legs against her sides. She wanted me to take my legs completely off of her, but I couldn't do that. I always ride with a little bit of calf pressure and she would just have to get used to it. She kicked at my leg a couple of times but I didn't change anything, and eventually she quit arguing. She didn't understand or know how to respond properly to any leg aids, but she allowed the leg to stay on, which opened the door for such conversations later.

During this entire time her head was up in the air, armed and ready for all sorts of bridle arguments, but I didn't go there. I knew she would not want to add going to the bit and connection to her list of compromises that day. I gave her a rough idea of what I would expect from her as far as connection was concerned, laughed at her when she argued, and then called it quits for the day.

The next lesson began the same way, but things improved dramatically. I worked a little more on the fact that she must submit to my requests (at least in a general way), and then we focused on some of the aids that would fine-tune the process. An opinionated little thing, at least twice during the ride she threw down on me, in a manner of speaking: that is, she balled up behind me, pinning her ears and looking backwards at me in what I'm sure she thought was an intimidating glare. I whacked her and gave her a sharp half-halt, and she backed down both times.

When she did give up on an argument and settled into a work pattern, she didn't hold a grudge or get resentful and sulky the way some horses do. Instead she was almost cheerful on the other side of a temper tantrum. This was a significant indicator. Considering that technically she had just lost an argument, I figured that some social tendencies and a more respectful attitude were not too far away.

Hey You and I had a wonderful show together. She learned something new each day, and, while she would still argue on occasion, she started to agree that it was okay for me to be in charge of her actions. As the days and rides went by, she began to act in a contented and somewhat easy-going manner. She finished second in a class of about seventeen in the Open Sport Horse Under Saddle mares division. Since she was a green four-year-old, in with Second and Third Level dressage horses, I thought that spoke volumes about her talent and trainability.

Hey You returned to Illinois with us and is now almost six years old. A pleasure to ride and train, she is working on all the First and Second Level movements. She still acts bossy sometimes and tries to assert herself, but she never gets away with it; she just does it because her character compels her to. My daughter

> ### KEEP CHALLENGING HORSES IN CHECK
>
> ▶ Believe that you must be the leader.
>
> ▶ Handle infractions fairly as soon as they arise.
>
> ▶ Don't get emotional.
>
> ▶ Dictate, don't argue.

Kassie, who rides her some of the time, has learned to ride cheerfully through such problems, and of course Hey You and I understand each other just fine.

CONCLUSIONS

Hey You was not a difficult horse either to train or to figure out. She was about a 4 on the aggressivity scale in terms of her challenging tendencies, and her social side best defined itself as a sense of humor or an interest in repairing relationships after an argument. That trait in particular would separate her from a strictly challenging type.

A clever individual, Hey You didn't mind the training process as long as the aids were well-timed and the dosage correct for the situation. When the mare did argue or disagree with a request, she was easy to correct because she was not in the habit of getting her own way.

The Challenging-Fearful Mix

The challenging-fearful horse is predominantly a challenging horse that at times borrows behaviors from the fearful personality. This type is not as self-confident as challenging horses normally are, and when handled fairly and correctly can become more attached to their trainers or handlers than a strictly challenging individual will. Their behavior at times may seem both testy and quirky.

The challenging-fearful horse could be described as a more complicated horse who may cause trouble even when aware and afraid of the repercussions. This type is best handled by a confident and empathetic horseman who knows when to be firm and when to be kindly and reassuring.

CASE STUDY: *Picasso*

Kim and I have a working student, Endel Ots, who is like a second son to us — both a fine rider and a wonderful person. Like my daughter Kassie, he has a natural talent for dressage along with a work ethic that is enviable in one so young. Consequently, he is further along on his riding journey than many professionals who are twice his age.

He originally came to us with his Friesian stallion Tjella S for training, and they both just stayed. Like many Friesians, Tjella S is a moderately social type. He and Endel are great together, and Tjella S is very forgiving of the inevitable mistakes that his rider has made and will continue to make on his way up the dressage ladder. Endel also had a project horse, a six-year-old red bay social-aloof Holsteiner gelding named Rohan, whom he was considering selling to buy a more talented FEI prospect.

Enter Picasso. Picasso was a recently imported eight-year-old Dutch Warmblood gelding, dark bay and 17 hands high. An amateur buyer from Indiana had imported him after viewing a videotape and paying for a vet check, and she was already regretting her purchase. She called to tell me that the horse was too much for her: he had bucked her off once already, and she described him as unsettled and argumentative (meaning that Picasso was looking for guidance and discipline and she was not providing it).

This can be a scary situation for an amateur to deal with, and she admitted he had made her quite timid. She fondly remembered riding Rohan at our place and said she would like to have a horse more like him. I told her to send me a videotape of the new guy, and I would see what we could do.

The videotape turned out to be the footage from Holland that she had originally viewed before she made the purchase. I wished I had seen it before she spoke for the horse because there was plenty of information suggesting that at this stage of his training he was not the right horse for a lower-level amateur rider. The talent was evident, but it was also clear to me that the schooling footage had been cleverly edited.

Picasso was a big, rangy, fairly supple FEI prospect showing some abilities for lateral work, passage, and lead changes. His rider in the videotape was an inordinately tall, skinny man who was doing a fairly effective job of making this somewhat rebellious horse look compliant and trained. He was riding Picasso through all the Fourth Level movements and some of the FEI work, but none of it would hold up under a judge's eye, which meant the horse was not ready to show at any of these levels. Although Picasso was impressive, he was clearly a bit of a handful and neither comfortable nor happy with the work he was being asked to do.

Although Picasso was impressive, he was clearly a bit of a handful and neither comfortable nor happy with the work he was being asked to do.

Endel watched the videotape with me and, being an enthusiastic idealist, thought the horse was fabulous. The notion came up that maybe a horse trade was in order: Rohan for Picasso. I was not against the idea. Rohan would be eminently suitable for the Indiana lady, and Endel (with our help) would look great on the big bay, certainly the more talented of the two horses. The trade took place and we began devising a training program to suit Picasso and Endel's journey toward FEI.

A quirky horse, Picasso liked to argue (almost reflexively) about the aids, yet he was afraid to be in trouble for his actions. He would initiate a misbehavior and then overreact or panic when he was corrected. His tricky personality may not have been taken into account in his previous environment.

It was clear there had been some shortcuts in his training program. Horses that end up in a sales barn in some European countries are not trained the same way they would be for competition or amateur use here. European sale horses must do FEI movements in order to be sold, and a skilled rider can train a horse in some of these maneuvers even when the animal's strength and education should not really allow it.

At any rate, Picasso did not fully understand everything that was expected of him, so it was back to basics in the snaffle bridle. Endel started with the Training and First Level movements, seeking the required calm, forward, and straight relaxation that was missing from the horse's program.

Picasso was testy. Once he learned how to argue effectively and block the aids, his challenging nature suggested this as an option during every ride. Endel quickly learned that quiet riding with clear, firm aids was the order of the day. He also learned never to let Picasso make him lose his temper. The few times that he did get frustrated or angry with Picasso's behavior and overdid a correction, Picasso would turn his testy responses into overreactive ones, running through the aids and leaping around athletically.

At first Picasso's difficult nature and his prior training were hard and frustrating for Endel to handle correctly. He was used to his forgiving Friesian allowing his mistakes of timing or accuracy in the aids, and Picasso was not nearly so tolerant of such shortcomings. It is amazing, however, what motivation, determination, and hard work will produce. Once Endel developed a workable game plan for Picasso and began to understand the differences in personality between his two horses, a working relationship emerged.

At their first show together in Orlando, Florida, they scored an impressive 68 percent at Third Level and earned the title of High-Scoring Junior Horse and Rider for the entire four-day show. The honor included the Edgar Hotz Memorial Trophy, a prize toward which Endel had aspired. He looks great on Picasso, and they are now making steady progress, on the right path toward a bright future as an enviable FEI partnership.

CONCLUSIONS

Picasso's challenging-fearful personality would be quite difficult for inexperienced riders to handle. He was a 4 or 5 on the aggressivity scale in terms of both his challenging tendencies and his fearful traits, whenever they showed up. Key indicators included:

1)   He argued with and overreacted to the aids.

2)   He panicked when corrected.

3)   He was intolerant of rider shortcomings.

Although Endel was fairly early into his horse-training journey when he acquired Picasso, he had the necessary riding skills to make progress with this potentially difficult type. Being part of a sound training program with experienced eyes on the ground was a crucial part of this particular success story.

It is important to note that because Picasso's dominant personality is challenging, he is not afraid of new things or unfamiliar environments the way many fearful horses are.

The Challenging-Aloof Mix

Though not the friendliest horse in the barn, the challenging-aloof type is found fairly often in many different breeds and disciplines, so it is wise to familiarize yourself with it. Depending on where an individual falls on the aggressivity scale, this type can range from mildly testy and disinterested to downright cranky and withdrawn. I have known quite a few horses of this type, but Harlow, my daughter Kassie's first horse, is the best example.

CASE STUDY: *Harlow*

moderately challenging

moderately aloof

When you are twelve and both your parents are horse trainers, you will inevitably clamor for riding privileges, even if your interest is short-lived. I never insisted that my children follow in my footsteps because, for me, riding was both a full-time occupation and a slightly tiring hobby. I had no interest in badgering reluctant children into something that would only mean more work for me.

Kassie, the third of my four wonderful children, had hung around and played in our horse-centered environment for her entire life, and at twelve she decided she wanted in. "In" meant working as a groom: cleaning stalls, grooming, bathing, tacking, feeding, and longeing, all in the hope of some riding time at the end of the day. Kassie earned her riding time and learned to ride (that is, she learned to get along with horses) relatively quickly.

*Kassie and Harlow
at Second Level.*

Kassie is unique in our family in that she has a certain light, effortless charm that both horses and people respond to and feel comfortable with immediately. My smiling and cheerful daughter went through her young life assuming that all creatures, whether two-legged or four-, would be her friend at the end of the day, and she was correct more often than not.

About this time our friend Sonja Vracko, a dressage judge and trainer, brought us a videotape showing a recently started twelve-year-old Dutch Warmblood mare, Harlow. Since her importation from Holland the dark bay mare had lived on a breeding farm out West, producing tiny dressage prospects, and now, later in life, she was reluctantly starting her career as a riding horse.

On the videotape she looked fairly obedient, albeit a little cranky. She was schooling all of the Training and First Level dressage movements with relative ease and seemed to be a good enough mover. She was also quite reasonably priced, due to her age and lack of experience, so we bought her as a possible mount for Kassie, knowing she would always have some value as a broodmare.

Anyone who was ever a twelve-year-old girl, or has had any experiences with one, can imagine the frenzy of excitement following the announcement that a new horse would soon be arriving at the farm, and that said equine was slated to be her first real project horse. Kassie was so wound up that Harlow could not have received a warmer welcome if she had been that year's Kentucky Derby winner.

- -

She kept her ears halfway back and seemed to scowl at everyone:
two signs of a moderately challenging horse. It was obvious to
Kim and me that she would prefer to be left alone.

- -

The mare, however, had other ideas. Granted, she was tired from her trip (that's what we told Kassie), but Harlow was not impressed with either the people or the fuss that surrounded her at Indian Hills. She kept her ears halfway back and seemed to scowl at everyone: two signs of a moderately challenging horse. It was obvious to Kim and me that she would prefer to be left alone. We pried Kassie away from her and let the mare settle in.

WORKING WITH A CHALLENGING-ALOOF MIX

Although Harlow could easily be called "cranky" or "moody" at times, she was never really mean or dangerous. We could tolerate her moodiness because she did not behave badly other than ear pinning, scowling, and showing irritability at having her girth tightened.

Kassie, the mare's main handler, had to try not to become discouraged by Harlow's somewhat cranky nature. She needed to focus on her horse's responses to actual aids and requests and not on her attitude toward them.

This lesson applies to all personality types. Be aware of attitude, but be sure to separate it from behavior. As a trainer you can address only behavior issues.

About a week after Harlow's arrival, Kassie caught up with me as I was walking through the barn and asked if I thought Harlow disliked her. She suggested I accompany her to the stall so I could see for myself. Sure enough, as Kassie approached Harlow's stall, calling and talking to the mare in a sing-song voice, Harlow pinned back her ears and scowled.

"See," Kassie said, "it's like she's always telling me to go away." I explained to her that it was nothing against her personally; the mare was just like that. I defined Harlow's personality for her and mentioned that she would be unlikely to change her characteristics very much. Kassie would have to learn to develop a working relationship with this grumpy type of horse if she wanted to enjoy any success, because this was Harlow's basic nature.

Kassie was so customarily cheerful herself that she had a hard time understanding why any creature would start the day with a scowl. Nevertheless, she redoubled her efforts. She was not about to be put off by a mare that would rather be retired early or have a few more babies than be Kassie's very own riding horse.

The more cranky and disinterested Harlow acted, the more amiable and determined Kassie reacted, until they developed a partnership. And while Harlow seemed determined not to let it show, she actually started to enjoy the girl's company.

It was now the beginning of summer vacation, and Kassie attached herself to that mare like a burr and charmed her way along. The more cranky and disinterested Harlow acted, the more amiable and determined Kassie reacted, until they started to develop a partnership. Kassie took Harlow on trail rides. She jumped fences with her, rode her bareback, even took the mare swimming in the pond that was out behind the barn. And while Harlow seemed determined not to let it show, she actually started to enjoy the girl's company and all the attention she received. She

Kassie and Harlow swimming in the pond.

scowled less, watched for Kassie with an almost interested look on her face (mostly because the girl always brought treats), and seemed to enjoy her grooming more. Harlow was brave and confident (which was great for Kassie), a fearless jumper, and absolutely safe on the many trail rides they took.

Harlow's aloof side started to come forward during this time of so much attention. Unlike a strictly challenging horse, who will interact or argue almost indefinitely as a matter of course, the mare had a rather narrow tolerance for such constant stimulation. She needed her alone time and soon made it clear to Kassie that if she didn't get it she would not be so agreeable on her next outing. Kassie compromised and quit fussing quite so much.

Over time the two became great show partners, winning many dressage tests and three regional championships. During the three years that they campaigned together, Harlow also found time to give us another foal. We bred her to the passively social Dutch Warmblood stallion Liberty and she produced a moderately social filly named Willow, who seems to have the best characteristics of each of her parents.

Harlow and Kassie made the journey up into Fourth Level together before the mare's talent and athleticism peaked. She is now back to broodmare duty, but the relationship that she forged with Kassie, while not entirely conventional, is still secure. When Willow was born, Kassie was the only human who enjoyed full access to the foal. We have pictures of Kassie and Willow sleeping on the floor of the stall together as Harlow stood watch over the pair.

Unlike a strictly challenging horse,

who will interact or argue almost indefinitely as a matter of

course, the mare had a rather narrow tolerance for such constant

stimulation. She needed her alone time.

Harlow was very valuable for young Kassie because she helped my daughter understand that all working relationships do not need to be smiles and roses. Some are built on determination, motivation, and the ability to see the positive side of everything.

CONCLUSIONS

Harlow gave me a good indication of her personality on the video-tape we viewed before purchase. Despite her nature, her earlier training had proceeded well. We trusted Sonja Vracko's assessment that while "moody" at times (a euphemism often used to describe challenging mares), she certainly wasn't dangerous. Here are three clues that emerged in our first days with her:

1) Often cranky, Harlow kept her ears pinned back and seemed to scowl when anyone approached.

2) She had a narrow tolerance for stimulation.

3) She was self-confident and brave under saddle.

The mare's personality was about a 5 on the aggressivity scale in terms of her challenging tendencies and slightly lower in terms of her aloof ones. She remained consistent about these traits for the time that we had her in our training barn and will likely be a broodmare for the remainder of her years.

PART FOUR

YOU & YOUR HORSE

Putting concepts into practice: how to

work with your horse's temperament,

learn your own personality preferences,

and match horse and rider

*If you needed to learn
something new, you would most likely
choose an expert whom you could respect
and feel comfortable learning from. Your
horse's needs are not that different from
yours. To learn from you he must trust and
respect you. To be most effective, you must
understand all you can about your horse's
personality, prior training, and physical
issues before you ask him to obey or relate to
you. My hope is that some of the following
tips will help guide and streamline
your training journey.*

CHAPTER ELEVEN

WORKING WITH PERSONALITY

THERE IS A SUCCESSFUL RECIPE FOR TRAINING each of the four personality types. Whether your horse is social, fearful, aloof, or challenging, there are small but key differences in how each type should be handled and corrected from birth or weaning on.

Keep in mind that even after you have identified his basic personality type, you still need to determine where your horse might fall on the aggressivity scale (see chapter 2). Each of the four types will have quieter or louder reactions to almost any situation, depending on whether the horse is passive, moderate, or aggressive in expressing his individual personality type.

By now you have undoubtedly realized that if you handle a fearful horse the same way you handle a challenging one, the horse will be in trouble. And if you handle a challenging horse the same way you handle a fearful horse, *you* will be in trouble. Handling and training a horse according to his personality type is paramount for true partnership and success. This section should not be interpreted as an all-inclusive training manual but more as a series of helpful tips and guidelines that will help you to understand and work with your horse's temperament.

It is always best, of course, if an individual horse's personality is taken into consideration from birth on, but unfortunately that does not always happen. I will start with weaning and describe how best to handle the four types from that time on. I believe that imprinting a newborn is a valuable expenditure of time, and there are many books on the subject, taking you into as much detail as you would like to go.

Other than imprinting, early handling is helpful but not mandatory. When you are dealing with an unweaned foal you must consider the personality of the broodmare as well, and often three is a crowd in a training situation. Sometimes it is better to wait and deal with the foal as an individual after he is weaned, especially if the mare is of a fearful or challenging nature. If your young horse will be handled by a variety of people, however, you will need to spend time interacting with and training your foals.

Training a Weanling

Since weaning is normally the first traumatic occurrence in a foal's short life, it is natural for a youngster of any type to act worried, frightened, and upset when initially separated from his dam. The differences among all of the types will be most evident after the foal has settled down a bit, post-separation, and starts interacting and responding to you.

Dos and Don'ts for Handling All Weanlings

When you start working with a young horse, always remember: this is the beginning of your foundation together. Young horses start out with no knowledge of their own. Build on that. Don't get impatient or set your expectations too high. Small increments of success are far better than arguments and confusion. Here are some tips to keep early lessons safe and effective.

LEADING. Most problems that arise from early leading practice begin with the handler approaching the initial lessons unsafely. The handler mistakenly pulls on the leadrope, either to restrain a wayward youngster or to try and drag him in a certain direction. More often than not, the handler gets kicked, run over, or stepped on.

Instead, when leading a youngster, stay close to his shoulder and restrain or guide him with direct half-halts (see next page). If the horse is very young or small you may need a butt rope and/or a helper. Pulling on a horse — either with the leadrope when he is young or later with the reins — does not work and may cause you to be kicked or dragged yourself, as well as setting undesirable precedents for future schooling and handling.

CORRECTING. Do not correct a biting horse by slapping or swatting him in the face. Challenging types will quickly turn this into a game they will exploit to their advantage. Instead, I push my fingernail into the muzzle of a horse who is trying to nip. Unobtrusive yet annoying, this soon puts him off the idea of biting.

If your youngster does not want to stand still, do not try to wrestle him into submission. Instead, walk forward and halt, then repeat, again and again, each time adding a half-second to your halt time. Soon your horse will stand still for a longer time.

Finally, remember that any horse can kick. Keep yourself out of position and be aware and observant of your horse's temperament, mood, and comfort zone at all times.

HANDLING. When handling a young horse, keep moving with him. Do not stand still and try to force him to behave.

APPLYING A HALF-HALT

A half-halt is a short, sometimes soft, sometimes sharp inter-
ruption of the connection on your lead rope, longe line, or rein.
Whether you are leading, longeing, or riding a horse, the basic
idea of a half-halt is still the same.

▶ A half-halt *always* begins and ends in softness. This means
that you should have a soft feel on the line, apply the half-
halt, and then immediately soften again.

▶ A half-halt should cause your horse to pause momentarily
and pay attention to you. His attention is the desired
response. After an effective half-halt you could apply
another to have the horse halt, or you could apply a driving
aid to have the horse move on again.

▶ A half-halt is similar to calling out your child's name *before*
you start barking orders at her. If a child is intently staring
at the television set and never acknowledges that you
even spoke, do you think she will accomplish your request?
Consider communication with your horse in the same
manner. You need the attention of your subject before you
can expect to achieve the desired response.

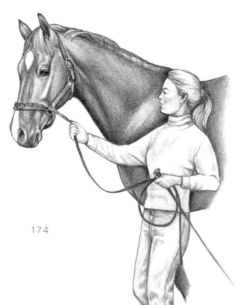

LEADING. Staying close
to the horse's shoulder,
apply a direct half-halt
(downward and back-
ward) and then softly
release. The lead line can
be under the chin, over
the nose, or hooked to the
bottom ring of the halter.

MOUNTED. All half-halts start and end in soft contact. When applying a mounted half-halt, use a two-rein direct aid that goes through your hips to the horse's hips.

LONGEING. Start from a soft connection, give a steady backward aid on the longe line, and softly release.

Weaning the Social Horse

The social horse may be one of the easier horses to handle at weaning time. You must be sure, of course, that he is weaned within a safe stall or pen in which he is unlikely to get hurt. Some people wean their youngsters by putting two weanlings together in one stall, and this works extremely well with most of the types. Remember, though, that you will still have to wean the two new friends from each other eventually, so sometimes it is better just to separate your youngsters right away and handle the weaning process all at once. You can turn the babies out together during the day, but then separate each into individual stalls whenever they are in the barn.

Social babies appreciate being visited and interacted with in general but especially during weaning time, when they may feel a little lost. Take time to socialize with your young horse so he does not become too lonely.

Be careful, however, not to let young social horses invade your space in a way that will be unacceptable when they are older and much larger. I knew of a teenager that let his Arabian weanling put his front feet on his shoulders every time he went in the stall with him. You can just imagine how dangerous that habit would become when the horse matured. Always think about how you would like your young horse to behave when he is older, and work toward that.

Your youngster should lead and handle quietly. If he did not learn to lead before weaning then it is the first order of business now. All young horses should be handled daily during weaning time: this is the foundation for all future training.

How much you decide to handle your social horse depends on the amount of time you have to invest and your individual expectations.

▶ Keep your lessons short and simple.

▶ Make your social horse stay attentive to you with small half-halts on his lead line that cease when he focuses and walks quietly beside you.

▶ Pet and groom your youngster, but do not let him invade your personal space by nosing you and molesting you for treats. All personality types must realize that you are allowed in their personal space but they are *not* to intrude in yours.

▶ Because your social horse enjoys interactions, talk to him and call his name when you pass by his stall.

▶ Let him know he is part of the program and give him turnout time (hopefully with some buddies his own age) and some handling time each day.

Most social horses are easily distracted. Whenever you work with your social youngster make him focus on you, no matter what other distractions are around. (See box on previous page.) Start to work on this potential problem now by ensuring that your little busybody pays attention to you.

CASE STUDY: *Jamie's Sidekick*

aggressively social

We had a little runt of an Arabian weanling that I got for free when I purchased five other Arabians, and my son, Jamie, who was only ten at the time, spent many hours with him. We called the colt "Weenie" and, rather unfortunately, the name stuck to him for a good long time. Jamie had nothing but time on his hands, so he spent hours working with the moderately social young colt. I gave him a few lessons, along with some safety dos and don'ts, and then monitored them from a distance.

Jamie took the colt for walks on a lead line as if Weenie were a big dog learning to "heel." Together they explored the woods, the marshy area behind our house, and the big fields that surrounded it. Jamie then concocted a little obstacle course for Weenie, and each day he introduced him to a new challenge. Within a few weeks the colt would negotiate a tire maze, back through some poles, walk over a tarp on the ground, and trot over a small jump. All of this was accomplished without anxiety or carrying on from the seven-month-old colt.

One day Jamie called me over to the side of the house, and when I rounded the corner I saw the two of them squeezed inside Jamie's clubhouse. It was a comical and ridiculous sight, but the colt was completely at ease in the cramped quarters because Jamie had taken the time to introduce him to so many new things. I laughed at them but did tell my son that he needed to keep Weenie out of the playhouse, no matter how content the youngster seemed to be.

Jamie and the colt remained great friends. Consequently, when it came time to start Weenie under saddle, Jamie went through the process with me step by step and was the first to ride and show his own project horse.

---

*All a weanling really needs to know is how to lead,
how to let his feet be handled, and how to stand for grooming.*

Few people have as much time and energy to commit to their weanling's initial handling as children like Jamie do, and the fact that the youngster was of a social nature made Jamie's job easy. Whatever amount of time you spend, you must always keep an eye on the future trainability of your horse. There are no absolutes on what a weanling really needs to know besides how to lead, how to let his feet be handled, and how to stand for grooming. Once you are comfortable that your social youngster can manage these simple tasks, he may be turned out in a group situation with less frequent handling until breaking time.

FEARFUL
TRAINING A WEANLING

When you start leading and grooming a young fearful horse, remember that reassurance is the name of the game. Proceed slowly, make your actions quiet but definite, and let your young horse gain confidence and security through you.

▶ Establish boundaries as you would with any other horse. (See Training a Social Weanling, page 177.) However, you probably won't need to be as firm with this type of horse as with other types if he does step out of line.

▶ If your young fearful horse stays away from the front of his stall or doesn't want to interact with others in a group, find him just one friend who is not a bully (a moderately or passively social horse would be ideal) and turn them out together.

▶ Coax him into interacting with the comings and goings in the barn aisle instead of hiding from them.

▶ Make sure any workers are aware of your youngster's personality traits so they don't scare him and set your progress back. Unsettling experiences seem to stick with a fearful horse for a long time, so proceed slowly and try to avoid them.

▶ Because fearful horses are more insecure and panicky than other types, they may injure themselves more frequently at weaning time. One more reason to take it slow and steady.

▶ Find professionals who are patient and experienced in dealing with young horses. Harsh or unpleasant treatment or handling by the veterinarian or farrier tends to stay with this type longer than others.

Put a hand up in front of the fearful horse and an elbow into his neck to keep him from crowding your personal space.

Weaning the Fearful Horse

Great care and caution must be applied to weaning a fearful horse, because this type is more prone to injury than others if he panics. Make sure the environment is safe, and use great care when you handle a newly weaned fearful horse so that you don't get hurt. When horses are afraid, especially young fearful ones, they may not pay attention to their environment or to the people around them. That means everyone else must watch out for them if they become frightened or too reactionary.

A fearful horse needs reassurance, stability, and routine. This will not change as he matures, so help him gain confidence in his world by treating him quietly and with great patience.

Even if you turn him out in a big group or stop handling him on a daily basis, be careful to reestablish the same routines when you do resume working with him. Familiarity will always be most important to a fearful horse.

ALOOF

TRAINING A WEANLING

You can never assume that an aloof horse is either paying attention or ready to react to you the way that the other personalities might. The aim of all your initial aids should be to make him either look at or focus his attention on you. At first, just this call to attention should be enough.

▶ Practice making your aloof youngster aware of you either by calling him, invading his space, clucking to him, or touching him in some way until he acknowledges you.

▶ While leading or handling him, give small half-halts on the lead rope until he gives you his attention, and then cease as soon as turns his focus toward you.

Whichever method you use to demand your aloof horse's attention, this very important first response should be instilled in him and periodically refreshed throughout his entire training process. After you have established a reliable way to seize your aloof youngster's attention, you can start to make some requests of him. Here are some strategies:

▶ While leading your aloof horse, ask him to halt by clucking or giving him some half-halts on the lead.

▶ When he tunes in to you, halt and give him a larger half-halt along with the voice command of your choosing.

▶ If your subject does not respond, repeat with a firmer half-halt until he does. Do not plant yourself and start pulling. Walk a few steps, halt, and apply a stronger half-halt.

▶ If the horse still does not respond, repeat the process with an even stronger half-halt. All horses will eventually respond to such patience and procedure.

Weaning the Aloof Horse

The process of weaning the aloof horse is often not too difficult, especially for a passive individual. When you start the handling process the aloof weanling may seem a little removed or slow to react or respond to you, and this is when the most important work should begin. The training problems that this horse will face now and through much of his training sessions will usually be due to his lack of focus and/or the attention he pays to the aids.

Start now. Create meaningful interactions with your horse based on the "one aid, one answer" theory (see box, page 188). Avoid quick or pointless interactions with your aloof weanling, which will overwhelm him and cause him to tune you out even more.

Once you have developed some sort of relationship pattern with your aloof horse, you can turn him out in a group situation with less frequent handling until it is time to start him under saddle.

Weaning the Challenging Horse

Weaning the passive or moderately challenging horse will not present too large a problem — at least the actual weaning part, anyway. Because challenging youngsters are usually quite confident, they typically settle in well once they recover from the initial trauma of losing their mothers. If your youngster has a more aggressively challenging nature (you will know this if he was bullying the other youngsters in his turnout or trying to bully his own mother before being weaned), then you have your work cut out for you.

Develop good habits with your challenging youngster early on, and always remember that respect is the name of the game: his respect for you and your respect for him. He must respect you and

CHALLENGING
TRAINING A WEANLING

Do not allow your challenging horse to interact with other horses while you are working with him. He will focus on trying to establish a pecking order or on intimidating any new horse and will therefore stop paying attention to you.

▶ The technique of "one aid, one answer" (see box, page 188) must be adhered to throughout the training life of any horse, and the answer can never be "no."

▶ Challenging horses not only enjoy saying no to a request, but they don't even seem to mind if an argument ensues. Do not argue with your challenging horse. Give him an order and then correct him if he does not comply.

▶ These are the least submissive of all the types, so you must establish yourself as the one in charge and be ready to remind your challenging youngster whenever necessary.

▶ Do not let your challenging horse invade your personal space, which I define as a one-to-two-foot circumference around myself. (Actually, no horse should be allowed to invade your personal space. It is just much more dangerous if a challenging horse develops that habit.)

▶ Reward your challenging horse for compliance, especially after you have had to establish a new boundary or he has been testy and hard to deal with. It is good for challenging types to realize that life is much better when they comply.

▶ Challenging horses have a strong sense of fair play, so never step over the line from correction toward cruelty.

▶ Do not assign too many handlers to your challenging horse, because he will test each one.

you must be fair toward him at all times. One of the best things about challenging horses is that they do understand the pecking order. If you establish yourself early on as the leader in your group of two, you will be on your way to a successful relationship.

Youthful challenging behavior can range from mildly testy to openly defiant, and you must be ready to deal with each infraction in the manner in which it was delivered. For example, a small infraction, such as trying to bite or grab the lead line out of your hand, needs a small reprimand; striking at you with a front leg, on the other hand, must be dealt with instantly and rather sharply. (See Reprimanding, below.) Challenging horses keep track of what they can get away with and seem to be constantly trying to add new ways to "one-up" their handlers in any given situation.

Much of the following advice in dealing with challenging horses is geared toward those that are a 4 and above on the aggressivity scale. The ones below that number will be easier to keep in line.

REPRIMANDING

You may wonder how best to reprimand a challenging horse. Always make the punishment match the offense, while keeping your own safety in mind at all times. Here are three suggestions:

1) If your horse tries to bite or kick you while you are beside him, keep his head turned slightly toward you so he cannot turn away and kick at you again. Make sure he has a lead line or something attached to him so he cannot just move at will.

2) Give him an open-hand slap under his belly.

3) Be ready to reprimand him again if he acts threateningly.

When reprimanding a challenging horse, keep your focus on him and be ready to handle any reactions to your corrections.

If you are not comfortable with this sort of interaction, find a trainer to deal with these issues so they do not get out of hand. Misbehaviors that are handled correctly and in a timely manner will soon disappear.

You will not have to wait long for most young or untrained challenging horses to initiate some sort of misbehavior, but you do not need to approach this type in a threatening manner. Your job is to handle any infractions as soon as they appear, not to provoke them. You cannot start arguments with a challenging horse. Fair requests that are fairly and firmly backed up are the key to success.

If you handle your challenging horse properly from the beginning, he will soon learn his place and become more trustworthy. If your horse seems to be quite high on the aggressivity scale (8 or above), then you will need to be vigilant that he does not develop any dangerous habits (biting, striking, kicking) before he is ready to start under saddle. Once a challenging horse gets away with such behavior he becomes progressively harder to correct later on.

Training Under Saddle

Once communication levels have been established and basic leading, handling, respect, and trust are intact, starting a young horse (while still a job for an experienced trainer) is not that difficult.

When we bring in a new horse, even if he has already been started, we usually take him out to the round pen to work on personality assessment and to see how he will interact one-on-one. We also use this time to assess how he responds to individual interactions such as half-halts, invasion of personal space, and restraint (tying). From there we devise an individual training program that will suit his needs. I have started many horses in my lifetime, with very good success, but my system isn't nearly as streamlined or effective as my husband Kim's. Consequently, he does all the initial round pen work, with help from our working students.

During the first thirty days of riding there is not that much that a youngster really needs to know. The essentials are: getting comfortable with the tack and equipment; tolerating a rider; and being willing to interact with the handler. Once those are accomplished the riding lessons are simple. Stop. Start. Steer.

Much of our initial riding is done in the round pen so we are not forced or tempted to steer our youngsters with the reins. Once they can steer reasonably well from an initiating rein aid followed by an outside leg at the girth, and they have a fair understanding of the half-halt, they can progress into a larger arena.

ONE AID, ONE ANSWER

It is important to understand, early on, a basic rule of horse communication — a rule that applies both on the ground and under saddle. Carol Lavell, a dressage Olympian, wonderful trainer, and my former coach, used to ask me the following question every time I overlapped my aids or allowed a horse to change the subject before he responded to a request. "Did you ask that horse to move off your leg?" she would inquire. When I answered yes, she would reply, in a slower and more enunciated way of speaking, "I didn't see him answer you!"

If you ask a horse to do something, anything, you must ask for only one thing at a time, and your horse must respond to each request. It doesn't even need to be the right answer: they simply need to respond. Once you receive a response you can ask for the next thing or change and refine your aid towards getting a different response.

For example, if I am leading a horse who is constantly lagging behind, I may take a short whip and tap him on the side. If he does nothing I will instantly tap him again, but this time a little harder. If the horse then overreacts and runs by me, I will not reprimand him because I just asked him to move and he did. I will refine my aids until I get the desired response, one aid at a time.

Training the Social Horse Under Saddle

Social horses are usually fairly simple to get started, provided you have a good system for doing so. The two rules for social horses will pretty much stay the same for their entire training process:

1) Social horses must be made to focus on you instead of everything else during their training time.

2) They must be made to understand and respond to the aids one at a time.

Social horses like and accept change well, but they may be a little too interested in their new environment to reliably respond to you. Don't take a young social horse who has worked entirely by himself and transition him directly into a crowded arena. Since he will be more interested in his atmosphere than he is in you, he may not respond to aids you thought he already understood. Remember that any horse, regardless of type, needs to focus before he can respond appropriately.

CASE STUDY: *Sonoma*

PASSIVE   AGGRESSIVE

1	2	3	4	5	6	7	8	9	10

passively social

Passively social horses are usually quite easy to get started, and if you don't ask too much too soon (and overstress them either physically or mentally), they usually make steady progress. We received a young Friesian cross in for training a few years ago. She introduced herself as a passively social type, uncomplicated in manner and actions. My understanding was that she was green-broke (which to me means started and comfortable with a rider but not yet trained), and because of her character, the footing in the round pen, and my busy schedule at that time, I skipped the round pen work and went right to the large indoor.

Indian Hills has a very large, at times crowded, and always distracting indoor arena. The sides open into the barn aisles, and there is another arena attached to the main one that always has something happening in it. I brought Sonoma into the middle of the large arena, climbed on her, and started riding. She was pretty unsure of the steering aids and had some trouble balancing in the canter, but overall responded and behaved very well.

When I called her owner to give an accounting of the ride, she interrupted me to ask, "Did you ride her already? She isn't broke yet." When I found out that I had been the first to back the mare, and I had walked, trotted, and cantered both ways in a busy arena, Sonoma's assessment went from good to exceptional. I am not saying that young horses should be started in such a manner, but this is the kind of mistake you could most likely get away with on a passively social horse.

CASE STUDY: *Limmerick*

Aggressively social horses can be time-consuming and at times exasperating to train. We have had more than a few of them in our barn. One example is a Dutch Warmblood stallion named Limmerick, nicknamed Glenny by his owner, Bob Oury. A beautiful dark bay with four white feet, Glenny is the class clown, the Bart Simpson and the Vinny Barbarino of any group he is in.

When we started with him as an early five-year-old, he didn't struggle with his attention span; he simply didn't have one at all. Everything, anywhere else, was much more fun and interesting to him than whatever we were trying to teach him that day. My husband, Kim, is a patient and methodical horse trainer, but he had his work cut out for him with this handsome and charismatic Dutch import. Along with Glenny's noteworthy lack of focus came absolutely no desire to even try to remember anything that resembled an aid sequence.

Bob, who owned the 1,000-acre farm where we worked and resided, as well as Glenny and four other imported stallions, had built some industrial-sized, rubber-sided round pens about eight feet tall. Because these formidable walls were impossible to see through or over, Kim decided to do much of the warmblood's early work in there.

Aghast at being shut away from all of the activity and commotion he thrived on, Glenny spent the first ten minutes on his hind legs straining to look over the tall walls. Resting one front foot on the side of the enclosure, he would stretch his long neck out to peer over the top. When his hindquarters eventually grew tired, he returned to all fours and glanced at Kim, standing in the middle of the round pen, to see if he had anything exciting to offer.

Kim had been waiting for this. He spent the next ten minutes teaching Glenny to come in and turn, using whip signals. When the young stallion's attention wandered away again Kim wisely called it quits and let Glenny off the hook for the day.

STARTING A SOCIAL HORSE UNDER SADDLE

▶ **Stage 1:** Social horses must be made to focus on you during their training time.

▶ **Stage 2:** They must be made to understand and respond to the aids one at a time.

▶ **Stage 3:** Be sure you have his focus before you introduce the social horse to changes in environment.

The next morning, Glenny repeated the previous day's efforts to look over and through the round pen walls. Then he looked at Kim for an instant as if to signal the onset of his attention span. Very soon after, Kim realized that the horse had retained very little from the previous day's interaction. He repeated the same lesson, and Glenny's mind wandered away again before they could proceed to any new material.

It was clear that Glenny needed time to mature. For the first year-and-a-half of training he did lots of short spurts of dressage interspersed with hours of trail riding and jumping. The stallion was an enthusiastic and exuberant jumper, leaping joyfully over anything that even looked like an obstacle.

After two years of fun and games, Glenny's attention span and work ethic have finally caught up with his abilities and talent. He is now working happily on the Third Level movements and still enjoys weekend trail rides with his owner.

*Let your social horse investigate
new surroundings to satisfy his curiosity.*

CONCLUSIONS

Typical of a young, aggressively social horse, Glenny had a very limited attention span for his work. Partly because of this, he needed and enjoyed variety in his lessons (jumping, trail riding, short spurts of dressage). The best and only approach with this type of horse is to wait for his maturity level to catch up with your work schedule and not to drill him too hard.

You can't take all the fun out of the work for a social horse. If you do, you run the risk of creating a robot instead of a partner.

First Outing on a Social Horse

Social horses usually enjoy new places and new experiences, provided they are not expected to do too much, too soon when they arrive. We had a young Friesian stallion in training named Boater, with a moderate to aggressively social character (about a 7 on the aggressivity scale).

Boater was delighted to go to his first dressage show. He was not in the least intimidated by this new atmosphere: "exuberant and interested" would have better described his attitude. Once we had unloaded the horses and set up the stalls with buckets, shavings, and hay, I had the working students longe the young stallion for a little while to rid him of excess energy. Then I climbed aboard and walked him all over the show grounds.

After about twenty minutes he stopped

trying to socialize with everyone, and at that point

I picked up the reins and put him to work.

He marched enthusiastically around the warmup arena, yelling out a greeting to every horse within earshot. I then let him stand at ringside and watch the other horses work, where he gladly surveyed the proceedings and called out randomly to the other animals he saw.

After about twenty minutes he stopped trying to socialize with everyone, and at that point I picked up the reins and put him to work. I was patient with his inattentiveness that day, but over the next few rides I gradually asked more and more from him in this new environment. By the third day of the show he was working as well in the show ring as he did at home, and I could not ask for more than that.

SOCIAL SUCCESS

There is no more rewarding sight at a horse show than that of a happy horse who understands and enjoys his work. Here are some suggestions for getting to that place with your horse:

- Keep the social horse's work easy enough for him to understand and to execute.
- Allow your social friend the freedom and flexibility to have some fun in his work.
- Make reasonable requests for focus and attentiveness, and then allow your social type some interaction or relaxation time during breaks or at the end of a ride.

I have seen too many people take a horse to a new place and start to bully him into compliance right away, without giving him a chance to settle in or satisfy his curiosities. This is hardly a recipe for success and will turn a potentially fun and rewarding experience into a sour and unproductive one.

SOCIAL PROGNOSIS

To sum it up, social horses are usually fun and rewarding to spend time with. They tend to tolerate, accept, and interact more easily than some of the other types do. A wide range of riders have been able to build successful training partnerships with social horses.

Training the Fearful Horse Under Saddle

Patience, patience, patience. When starting a fearful horse under saddle, you must leave your timetable at home. It takes as long as it takes, and patience is the name of the game. Be aware that a proper start for a fearful horse is more important than with any of the other types. Hard-won confidence is easily lost if you make hasty or foolish mistakes. Fearful types need to be comfortable with every single procedure related to their initiation into becoming a riding horse.

Assume that this type of horse could be afraid or unsure of just about anything, and then start from there. First, spend time making your fearful horse comfortable in the round pen or arena in which he will be working. Lead him around in there, and longe him, without tack, in both directions until he is familiar and comfortable with the workspace. This may take days, and it doesn't matter. Your horse's comfort level with each step of the process will be your green light to go on to the next step.

TACKING UP THE FEARFUL HORSE

Often I will introduce the tack for the first time to a fearful horse in the stall, as long as he doesn't become too claustrophobic in the confined space. If this is done slowly, bit by bit, over a few days, this type will soon get used to a saddle and bridle. Reassure and praise him often; it will pay off in your future relationship.

When you first saddle a fearful type, have another handler help hold or steady him so he cannot jump around before the girth is secured. Always keep a hand on the fearful horse when he is first saddled, rather than just letting him go in the stall or round pen.

STARTING A FEARFUL HORSE UNDER SADDLE

Have an assistant with you when you begin working with this type, and especially when you first mount up and ride. (While it is smart to have an assistant when starting any horse, it is mandatory with fearful types.)

▶ **Stage 1:** Allow your fearful horse the time to become familiar and comfortable with the round pen or arena where he will be working. Lead him around and longe him without tack in both directions.

▶ **Stage 2:** Introduce tack for the first time in the stall, piece by piece.

▶ **Stage 3:** When he is comfortable with the tack and the work environment, mount and dismount a few times and then end the first riding lesson.

▶ **Stage 4:** Continue to practice in the smaller pen until the responses to the half-halt, halt, and steering aids are consistent.

▶ **Stage 5:** Slowly introduce him to any new work environment.

Remember: Never rush a fearful horse, and do not get impatient with him. Instead, reassure and praise this type often.

Keep a reassuring hand on a fearful horse during initial tacking.

By controlling his movement you can ensure that he won't panic and scare himself even more.

Remember that this type needs first to accept and then to become comfortable with each new piece of equipment. Only then can he relax into the whole training process. It may seem time-consuming, but slow and steady truly is the quickest way to train a fearful-type horse.

First Ride on a Fearful Horse

Once your horse is comfortable with his arena and the equipment that will be used to ride him, you can start the riding process. Always have someone on the ground when you prepare to mount this type for the first time. Sometimes it is good just to mount and dismount a few times on the first day without proceeding any further, even if things go well. Then let the horse go back to his stall and process the experience. Never rush a fearful horse, and do not get impatient with him. If he gains comfort under saddle during the first few rides, you will be well on your way to starting a positive riding relationship.

This is one type that I may keep in the round pen until the responses to the half-halt, halt, and steering aids are confirmed. A fearful horse needs to gain security and confidence from his rider, so consistent, quiet, clear, and fair aids need to be established early. When you are ready to move to a bigger ring, longe or lead your fearful horse around before mounting, until he is no longer worried about the change in the work environment. Sometimes I will just sit on a young fearful horse in the arena, without asking anything of him, while I teach my other students, so he can assimilate the environment for a while.

CASE STUDY: *Rosie*

PASSIVE   AGGRESSIVE

| 1 | 2 | 3 | 4 | 5 | 6 | 7 | 8 | 9 | 10 |

aggressively fearful

I had an aggressively fearful Arabian mare a number of years ago. Although tricky to get started, she finally settled in to a comfortable training routine. Her story follows.

Back in my single-mom days, while I was training problem horses in Eustis, Florida, I picked up six Polish Arabians to break, train, and then resell. They were inexpensive because the breeding farm they came from was having a dispersal sale. The oldest of the group was a rose-gray mare that was nearly four years old.

Rosie was the hardest of the batch to deal with, by far, because of her personality, but she was beautiful to look at: movie-star, super-model-of-the-horse-world beautiful. Her finely sculpted face could easily have inspired an artist or a poet. The set and shape of her eyes, the way her head joined onto her neck; I can't do her justice, but you get the idea. She was a lot easier to look at than she was to handle, at least in the beginning.

Because Rosie was aggressively fearful and extremely fragile-minded when we met, every little thing was a big deal to her. All the other horses I had acquired at the time were already broke and going nicely under saddle (a few of them had even been sold) before Rosie even got started. I considered her one of those "take it slow and easy" projects.

I started by ponying her (leading her from another horse) beside my good trail horse, all around my property, just to build her confidence. Tacking, longeing, long-lining: these activities all required triple the usual time because of Rosie's very shallow comfort zone. I sensed, though, that she would be fine eventually, patience and time being the main requirements for success.

I was longeing her in my front field one afternoon when my blacksmith, Mel, stopped by. He inquired about my new horses, and I gave him a brief rundown and then explained that Rosie was the only one I hadn't backed yet. He offered to hold her while I climbed on and off a few times and I accepted. In those days I rarely had any help at all, so an extra set of hands was welcome.

Although I had not planned to ride her that day, she was tacked in a saddle, a bridle without reins attached, some side reins, and a longe line. I removed the side reins, tightened the girth and, with Mel holding on to the line, mounted up. Occasionally when you get on a horse, especially a green or a cold-backed one, you sense that they are poised for explosion. That filly was exactly that. She crouched down a little and froze in place, her back tight, holding her breath, just waiting to explode.

The farrier, Mr. Oblivious, picked up none of these signals. As I was preparing to dismount, pet, and reassure the nervous filly he said, "She seems fine, let's have her walk a few steps." Before I could respond or dismount, he tugged the filly forward.

Now she was loose, with a longe line dragging behind and tangling with her legs, and me, sitting helplessly on top, having no reins with which to stop or steer her.

Rosie came unglued. She leaped forward, and when she hit the end of the longe rope she started bucking and thrashing like a fish on the end of a line. Mel then made his second mistake and let go of the rope. Now she was loose, with a longe line dragging behind and tangling with her legs, and me, sitting helplessly on top, with no reins with which to stop or steer her. I reached forward and grabbed the crownpiece of her bridle, trying to gain some control, but she shook her head wildly and plunged forward at a greater speed.

As she gained momentum she started eyeing my front fence, a wire field fence with a 2-by-6 painted rail on top. She ran at it as if she planned on jumping or running through it, and at the last second she swerved. I fell into the fence or, more accurately, I bounced off it, breaking the board with my back and embedding the wire pattern along my side.

THE FEARFUL HORSE AWAY FROM HOME

Arrive early at your first show with a fearful horse.

▶ Bring his own feed and water buckets from home.

▶ Use your customary warmup routine at the show.

▶ Keep the atmosphere calm, predictable, and comfortable.

If you are new to showing or lack confidence yourself, have your trainer or a more skilled competitor ride your fearful horse the first few times.

I knew nothing was broken but I was banged and cut up some, and my side hurt a lot. Although I wasn't badly injured, I sensed the filly's confidence in me had taken a huge nose-dive, and for that I was mad. I ordered the blacksmith off my farm and told him to wait for an invitation before he stopped by again. I went over to Rosie, who was standing under my one tree in the corner of the field, shaking and sweating terribly. I pulled the tack off her and left her alone while I went to change my ripped clothes and assess the damage to myself.

Within a half-hour I was back out with the filly. Since this incident was a setback for her training, I wanted to get back on an even playing field with her. I brought her to my crossties, hosed her off, groomed her, and re-tacked her with a longeing surcingle and bridle. I reattached her side reins, longed her a little bit, and then put her away for the day.

The next day I tacked her wearing riding gear, longed her again, and then mounted her. I kept the left rein fairly short when I got on so that when she did try to leap forward she ended up in a small circle. I got on and off her ten times that day, and again the next. Within a week I could ride her around my front field with minimal trouble. Although she was still nervous, she was learning a pattern of behavior that was within her comfort zone. As long as I stayed inside these tentative boundaries, she allowed me to make progress.

I had Rosie for more than a year and I babied her pretty much the whole time. As her confidence in her work program increased, she became quite reliable about any riding situation that fell within her experience and comfort zone. She was cautious and reserved about new riders, but over time even her acceptance of these got stronger.

Rosie was eventually sold to a teenage riding student of mine who was almost as pretty as the mare herself. After I explained how she needed to be handled and ridden, Kristen, a fairly skilled and confident rider, took some lessons on Rosie until they were comfortable together. She loved the mare and would spend hours grooming and doting on her, activities the mare enjoyed.

Kristen was not an ambitious rider, not wanting to show or campaign the mare, and she didn't mind staying within Rosie's comfort zone when under saddle. The mare blossomed and grew even more beautiful, and over time they proved to be a good match for each other.

First Outing on a Fearful Horse

Although fearful horses can make wonderful show partners, remember that even once they are comfortable and working well in their training environment, there is likely to be some stress when you take them somewhere new. Always consider a fearful horse's basic lack of confidence when encountering new things, and let that awareness govern your actions.

Arrive early at your first show with this type of horse, spending whatever time is necessary in helping him settle into his new stall and environment. If possible, bring his usual feed and water buckets from home. That which is familiar will promote confidence.

Fearful horses like routine. In the weeks before a first show, establish a warmup routine that you can take with you and use to help your horse relate to his new environment. Do everything possible to establish a nonthreatening atmosphere for your horse. If these first few outings are handled properly and your fearful horse can feel comfortable and secure away from home, you are on your way to developing a positive show relationship with him.

As you help your horse assimilate new experiences and environments, it is imperative that you act confident and supportive at all times. If you are nervous or anxious about the competition or your horse's behavior, he will sense this and his own comfort level will be compromised. If you are new to showing or not that confident yourself, have your trainer or a more skilled competitor ride your fearful horse for his first few outings. Let the first few shows be all about the horse, his comfort level, and his future confidence, which will have a solid foundation if everything goes well.

CASE STUDY: *Diamond*

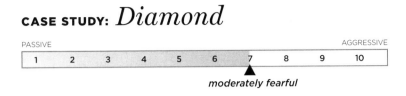

PASSIVE   AGGRESSIVE

1	2	3	4	5	6	7	8	9	10

moderately fearful

Diamond was a fearful Thoroughbred that I picked up off the racetrack as a late three-year-old, intending to make him into an event horse. I took him to a local show, just to accustom him to the environment, and rode him through a couple of rail classes.

At the end of the class, when we were asked to line up side by side in the middle of the arena, Diamond must have had a flashback to his racing days. The last time he had been lined up with a group of horses, all with riders on, he had been in the starting gate at the track. He waited about two seconds, then bolted forward out of the line, almost capsizing the judge and ring steward in the process.

Luckily, I sensed his intentions a half-second before he acted on them. I was too late to stop him but not too late to stay with him, reel him back in, and bring him back to the line with good humor and reassurance so he could try again to stand. He soon regained some composure and settled in, but if I had handled things less empathetically I could have created future problems.

By the time I sold him some months later, Diamond had become a confident and skilled event horse, and anyone who saw him tackle a cross-country course would have been hard-pressed to identify him as fearful. His introduction to jumping had been meticulously handled, and he bloomed with the confidence he had in his new rider.

FEARFUL PROGNOSIS

As stated earlier, fearful horses require a great deal of patience. They are worth the effort, however, because they want and need confidence so badly that they are grateful to those who can handle their fear appropriately. I enjoy building a relationship with fearful horses and have never been disappointed by the process.

Training the Aloof Horse Under Saddle

The aloof horse is usually a fairly straightforward training project. The passively aloof horse is typically one of the easiest types to start (about on a par with a passively social horse). In dealing with any aloof horse you can never assume that you have his attention. You must constantly check in with him and make him check in with you. Hopefully you have developed certain aids on the ground to get and keep your aloof horse focused on you, and this same process needs to be carried forward into the under-saddle work.

From the beginning, when training this type, you must keep accurate track of when you have gained or lost your project's attention. Many aloof horses will travel around with their ears fixed forward, seemingly intent only on ignoring you. Aloof types will often go to great lengths to ignore any kind of stimulus, and this sort of behavior cannot be tolerated. Every few strides, any horse (particularly an aloof one) should put an ear toward you, just to check in, and if he doesn't, "getting his ear" is job number one.

Once you have established a communication pattern between you and your aloof horse using the aids, you are on your way to developing a productive riding relationship. When training and riding issues come up (and they will, regardless of what personality

*If your aloof horse is avoiding the aids or staring off into space,
apply direct half-halts until you get his attention.*

Soften and reward as soon as he submits.

type you are riding), think first of the character of the horse, because this will often lead you to the cause of the misbehavior.

For example, an aloof horse may shy or startle while you are riding him, when you know very well that he has not previously been frightened of the particular monster that is suddenly spooking him. This is classic aloof disassociative shying, stemming from the aloof horse's need to try to avoid or break his connection with you. In this sort of circumstance it is wiser to be sure your horse is on the aids (connected to you and ahead of the leg) than it is to stop and reassure him.

Aloof horses don't need a lot of reassurance. They are rarely truly scared. They need connection: not hanging or pulling reins but an alive, connected rein that they must respond to and stay aware of during their active work time. A good reward for an aloof horse who has stayed attentive for some time is to stop for a moment and remove all rider-induced stimuli. Let the horse stand still and zone out for a moment before you resume more connected work.

First Outing on an Aloof Horse

When you first bring your aloof horse to a new environment, he is likely to settle in with relative ease. These individuals usually handle stall, feed, even handler changes fairly well. The main thing you need to keep in mind is that you want your aloof horse to pay attention to you and your aids, especially when it is time for your class. Once in a while I have found that an aloof horse may become slightly overstimulated by his new environment and therefore incapable of paying attention to his rider and the aids at the appropriate time.

STARTING AN ALOOF HORSE UNDER SADDLE

Try not to be too demanding with your aloof horse's attention span when you first work him at a new place. Here are some suggestions.

▶ Longe the horse for fifteen minutes, insisting that he tune in to you and connect only for the last five (leaving him ten minutes of "whatever" time).

▶ Do the same when you first mount, letting him take in or ignore whatever stimuli he wants, and then pick him up and demand his full compliance for slightly less time than you would at home.

These small compromises should help your aloof horse make good use of his developing interaction skills without overstimulating him, which would then cause him to withdraw from the whole experience.

Aloof horses are good for many types of riders, from beginner to advanced, but in order to be truly successful with one, you must understand and work with his need to avoid interactions whenever possible. Take the information about how to handle the aloof horse as a weanling (pages 182–183) and incorporate it into your training and riding program.

CASE STUDY: *Nimbus*

PASSIVE   AGGRESSIVE

| 1 | 2 | 3 | 4 | 5 | 6 | 7 | 8 | 9 | 10 |

aggressively aloof

A number of years ago we had in our stable an aggressively aloof Swedish Warmblood named Nimbus. He had learned to misbehave in the arena not because he was scared, angry, or having fun, but because when he presented a prolonged disobedience the judge would ring him out and he wouldn't have to compete at all. He did it as a sort of routine, just a little song and dance he would rather apply himself to than his dressage test. His previous rider had become frightened and confused by his misbehaviors and that is why we had him. Often, because of the timing of his shenanigans, I would get the feeling that he had removed himself mentally from the very disobedience he was actively participating in!

I fixed that problem at our first show together. When I went around the outside of the dressage ring before the bell rang to start the test, I asked the judge if she would please allow me to stay in the ring and finish my test. When Nimbus did misbehave I stayed in the show ring, made my corrections, and insisted he proceed through all the movements of the test. Although he cut up quite a bit, barging around, trying to run out the gate, and committing all manner of bridle crimes, I stayed on task, continuing to correct him. By the end of the ride he had submitted. Even though that test score was awful, the next test was 20 percent better because he had quit his carrying on.

Once Nimbus realized he would not get out of the ring early for bad behavior, he settled down and started to work during his

TUNING IN TO AN ALOOF HORSE

If your horse is tuning you out or avoiding interaction, you must develop some methods of regaining his attention that are reliable but streamlined and efficient. Some tips:

▶ Give a soft squeeze with the inside rein or use your inside leg at the girth in order to capture your mount's attention.

▶ If he puts an ear on you and seems to ask "What is it?", proceed with your next small request.

▶ If he does not respond at all, intensify the aid until you have your desired answer.

At all costs, avoid nagging (repeatedly applying the same aid at the same level of intensity). Nagging will just make an aloof horse dull, allowing him to ignore and tune you out even more.

rides. He still had training issues, but he quit trying to manipulate and control his ring time.

This is not to suggest that all your training issues be worked out in the show ring, because that is not acceptable and judges frown on such actions. However, problems that originate in the show arena usually need to be corrected in the same sort of environment, even if it means setting up a mock show for just that specific purpose.

ALOOF PROGNOSIS

Aloof horses are usually fairly straightforward training projects. Nevertheless, I have observed that often they do not reach their full physical potential because of their tendencies to disconnect from vital small communications between themselves and their riders. This one thing (the disassociation issue), when properly addressed by consistent rider connection, does more to ensure a productive future for the aloof horse than any other.

Training the Challenging Horse Under Saddle

The challenging horse can range from a fairly straightforward training project (the more passive individual) to a potentially difficult or dangerous one. The right knowledge and a good game plan are the best remedy for either.

If you have a challenging horse to start and you are not a horse trainer, consider hiring one for this job unless the horse is a 4 or below on the aggressivity scale and you are a fairly skilled and confident rider with clear thinking and good timing. If you do hire a trainer, however, not just anyone will do. Some trainers are actually afraid of horses (it sounds unlikely, but it is a fact), and you want to make sure you don't put your challenging horse with someone who is going to make matters worse for you down the road.

The initial starting process for training a challenging horse is more important to future success than it would be for any of the other personality groups (especially as far as personal safety is considered). More than any other type, this horse must learn to respect space and authority as he is first being introduced to the riding process. If your initial ground work has been correctly applied, this

STARTING A CHALLENGING HORSE UNDER SADDLE

▶ **Stage 1:** Never allow your challenging horse to think it is acceptable to deny or argue with a fair request.

▶ **Stage 2:** Challenging horses need more direction than reassurance as you initiate each new training step.

▶ **Stage 3:** Do not let a challenging horse think that it is permissible to "argue" with a request by, for example, scowling, ear pinning, kicking at the leg, or pulling on the reins.

type should never have a chance to realize that he does not need to comply with every request his handler or rider may make.

This is not to imply that a challenging horse will need rough or harsh treatment in order for you to gain the upper hand. It just means that your working relationship will be far more productive if your challenging horse never thinks it is acceptable to deny or argue with a fair request. If these boundaries are achieved and maintained during the initial riding process, they will lay the groundwork for all future success.

Kim and I have started many challenging types, ranging from passive to aggressive, all with good success. Both of us would much rather start our own challenging horses than fix up a job botched up by someone else. Regardless of type, when we do start our own horses, they have always made much more consistent progress than those we have had to correct or restart. This only goes to prove the age-old theory that the best chance you will have to influence or change any horse's behavior is usually the first one that you get.

The main thing that goes wrong when training a challenging horse is that this type may feel compelled to argue with a request, rather than comply with it. Each and every small request that goes unanswered then leads toward the next one being that much more difficult to achieve. Don't ask for too much with a challenging horse during the early stages, but do be sure to get what you ask for.

Because challenging horses are usually fairly confident, they need more direction than reassurance as you initiate each new training step. As always, it is essential to stay focused and pay attention to the small signals and interactions from your horse. This feedback your horse sends out will serve as the guideline for your next move. Training and riding a horse is like a conversation. Both parties need to pay attention in order to respond appropriately and at the right time.

First Outing on a Challenging Horse

Challenging types are usually paying attention to new things. Since they are fairly confident horses, not prone to panic, reassuring them in a new or strange environment is rarely necessary. What they do need to learn, early on, is that the respect and the rules that are important at home are equally important when they are away. When you first take your challenging horse to a show, try to arrange for an end stall or one with a tack stall on one side. This will help if your horse is kicking the walls or threatening a strange horse beside him, making someone else's show unpleasant (this usually only happens with more aggressively challenging horses).

Unless you have entered your horse in a race, where all that counts is attitude and speed, do not overface your horse during his first time in a new environment. Working at a show below the level expected while training at home is a wise strategy for any horse, but particularly for challenging types. Different types will respond in different ways, but a challenging horse may decide to test you if you ask him for his very best effort in a new environment.

Rather, let him do a class that is relatively easy, where he won't be constantly testing your authority and need to be microman-aged. If he does test your authority, you will have to handle it with a successful outcome in mind or you will set a precedent for more troubles to come. You can always count on a challenging horse to keep track of any infractions he thinks he has gotten away with and to try them again with increasing frequency.

CASE STUDY: *Indio*

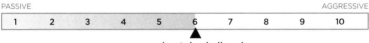

PASSIVE   AGGRESSIVE

| 1 | 2 | 3 | 4 | 5 | 6 | 7 | 8 | 9 | 10 |

moderately challenging

Many years ago I received a six-year-old chestnut-and-white Paint stallion in for training. The owner (afraid to give me the whole story) said he just needed a tune-up on some basic Western Horse-manship issues and committed him for one month of training. The young stallion, whom I quickly pegged as a very spoiled and mod-erately challenging individual, misbehaved at every opportunity. Before I had even mounted him once, he had tried to bash me with his head, kick at me, slam sideways into me, and bite everything I put near his face including the bridle, the halter, and myself.

I dealt with these infractions one at a time, firmly standing my ground but being careful to keep my own safety in mind. I side-stepped him when I had to, whacked him under the belly with an open hand more than once, and when leading him put the chain over his nose in order for my half-halts to have an effect.

I figured the riding evaluation would be just as full of conflict and carry-on, and it was. Within sixty seconds of being mounted — the moment I made my first steering request — he stood on his hind legs and walked deliberately for the gate leading back to the barn. He had to "touch down" a few times on his way but most of the trip was made on his hind legs.

When he neared the gate, I spun him hard and whacked him with the crop to get his feet moving. When he balked and tried to go up again, I took his head sharply to the right and whacked him again. Every time his feet were on the ground he was pressed to move forward *now*. Once he was in motion I urged him on until it was impossible for him to focus on anything but moving his feet.

As soon as I started to let him slow down he immediately tried to seize control of the situation by finding a way to rear again. I repeated the "turn and go" correction until he was tired enough to take a rest in the middle of the arena with me on board. I dismounted from there and took him back to the barn.

The next day he tried me again, but his heart wasn't in it and I had him under control within a few minutes. I talked to his owner later that day and she acted surprised. "Did he do that?" she exclaimed. "That is *so* unusual for him."

I informed her that her stubborn and spoiled six-year-old had not invented his wide-ranging repertoire of infractions and misbehaviors when he met me. It was evident by his confident and continuous attempts to control the situation that he had previously found ample reward through behaving in such a manner. I told her he would be much better within a week, but that if she wanted to ride him she would need to take a few lessons with me before she took him home.

The stallion was wise to her and started to

bully her as soon as she came within range.

He did improve, and three weeks into his one-month stay you would think he was a different horse. No more biting and carrying on in-hand, and I could ride him either in the arena or out on the trail without mishap.

When his owner came for her lesson, however, things went south in a hurry. The stallion was very wise to her, and although he had not tried to nip me for weeks he started to maul and bully her as soon as she got within range. The owner kept changing her response to him and backing away with little shrieks, which seemed to egg him on even more.

Before she mounted I requested that she listen to me and do exactly what I said, as soon as I said it. Unfortunately, she did not or could not. She was on that stallion less than a minute when he stood on his hind legs and started marching for the gate. The lady was shrieking and could not hear or concentrate on anything I said. When he triumphantly made it to the gate she slithered to the ground and said weakly that he must need more training. I climbed on his back, gave him one whack, and rode him for twenty minutes without a hitch.

After I was finished I informed the owner that this problem — the one between the two of them — was unsolvable in the present circumstances. She should sell the stallion, give up the idea of riding him, or enroll in a serious riding program to learn some necessary skills. A few days later she sent a trailer to bring the horse home. I never heard of them again after that.

Challenging horses such as this one may behave very differently with different individuals. Furthermore, this type is opportunistic: they won't behave themselves tomorrow just because they complied today. They need to respect a system, and each individual within that system, in order to approach anything resembling trustworthy behavior. This is especially true if they have been spoiled or behaved badly in the past.

CHALLENGING PROGNOSIS

In sum, challenging horses can be very charismatic and dynamic mounts. They can also be testy and trying. They are best handled by someone with clear thinking and good timing. When raised correctly and handled appropriately, challenging horses can excel at a variety of disciplines.

CHAPTER TWELVE

DEFINING TYPE WHEN CHOOSING A HORSE

WHEN YOU LOOK FOR A NEW HORSE, it is very important to make every effort to define the personality type of the individual you are considering. I recommend that you study the previous chapters carefully before you begin your search.

Defining type takes keen observation and the ability to categorize the information correctly. This may sound obvious, but you must clear distracting thoughts and feelings from your mind in order to accurately see what is in front of you instead of what you want to see or what someone else is telling you to see. When you are inexperienced at defining type, it may seem difficult; you may not notice enough details to help you make a fair evaluation. Rest assured, everything improves with the right kind of practice, and this skill is no exception.

If you visit your prospect with a trainer, understand that many professionals already know and define type to some degree in their daily work. Some do it instinctively; others through years of exposure or experience. Arm yourself with their expertise, but continue to improve your own personality assessment or "typing" skills. I'll walk you through the process in this chapter.

Once you know that a horse has suitable conformation and/or gaits for your intended purpose, then look at temperament. Even if everything else is superb, personality type may prove an important win-or-lose factor in your ability to succeed with this horse. If your horse is a competition or resale prospect and will be in full training with a competent individual who will do all or most of the riding, then it is probably more important that your trainer is comfortable with the horse's personality than that you are. However, if you will be the rider (whether right away or two years down the road), you should know what personality type you are buying. Remember that the more skilled you are as a rider, the greater the range of personality types you will be able to handle successfully.

When you shop for a new horse, try to avoid visualizing the kind of rider and competitor you want to become and then buying a horse for that person. Buy a horse that suits you right now, one that you want to work with and feel you will be able to connect with and relate to in your daily riding sessions.

The Initial Visit

Let's say you have made arrangements to see a horse that, through videotape, advertisement, or word of mouth, seems a likely candidate. If you can, bring your horse trainer or a knowledgeable friend along with you. Plan to take notes and possibly some video footage of your prospect. Make sure the sellers will let you watch the horse in the following ways, which we will discuss one by one:

- In the stall
- Being tacked and groomed
- Being longed and ridden
- Turned out (by himself and/or with another horse)
- Being fed

GETTING TO KNOW YOU

Early in this process it becomes useful to assess your own personality and your strengths and weaknesses as a rider. A realistic evaluation of the attributes you already possess and those you need to acquire is beneficial if not mandatory for success.

If you are not familiar with your own personality type I recommend that you take the Myers-Briggs Type Indicator (MBTI®). It is the most widely used temperament sorter in the world today and can give you a detailed profile of your basic and general personality preferences. Kim and I encourage all of our students and prospective horse shoppers to discover their type so that we can teach and help them more effectively. You will find some personality assessment guidelines, based on the Myers-Briggs system, on page 246–249, which you can use to start to define your personality type.

When you observe and then handle the horse, pay attention to his facial expressions, body language, and ears. Close observation is key to getting to know any horse. Keep your eyes open and pay attention to every detail. Bring a pen and paper and take notes.

As you observe the horse, assign a number from 1 to 10 to indicate how passive (quiet) or aggressive (loud) he is about each quality. This is not an exact science, so guessing at two different numbers if you are not sure is fine.

IN THE STALL

The horse should be loose in his stall when you approach with the seller. Ask how long the horse has resided here and how long he has lived in this stall. A horse that has lived in the same environment for more than a few weeks should be relatively settled in his environment. If he does not appear settled make a note of it.

How does the horse react when you approach his stall? Does he appear:

A) Alert and interested in your approach?

B) Cautious or wary?

C) Disinterested (nose in corner, no acknowledgment)?

D) Unwelcoming or surly?

On a scale of 1 to 10, rate the horse's passive or aggressive behavior.

TACKING UP

Observe the handler's interactions during the tacking process.

Is the handler:

A) Friendly and relaxed?

B) Quiet and reassuring?

C) Matter-of-fact (no special attachment or significance)?

D) Authoritative and/or controlling?

Is the horse:

A) Composed, relaxed, and attentive?

B) Slightly uncomfortable, wary, or ill at ease?

C) Withdrawn or disinterested?

D) Testy, threatening, sullen, or belligerent?

On a scale of 1 to 10, rate the horse's passive or aggressive behavior.

ASSESSING A HORSE IN THE STALL

SOCIAL. *Observe this horse's interested, alert expression.*

FEARFUL. *Note the twitching ears and worried look in the eye.*

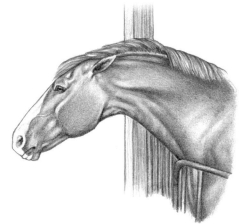

ALOOF. *Detached and disinterested, this horse does not welcome company.*

CHALLENGING. *This horse has a threatening facial expression, his ears are back, and he is pressing on the stall gate.*

223

LONGEING

It is important to watch the horse be longed, even if he does not go in side reins or any tack at all. This is a telling stage between the barn and the riding work. Does he:

A) Try to clown around, play, and call to equine friends?

B) Appear careful and attentive, or spooky and worried?

C) Seem detached and removed but obedient?

D) Act belligerent, overly confident, threatening, or surly?

On a scale of 1 to 10, rate the horse's passive or aggressive behavior.

UNDER SADDLE

While under saddle, does the prospect:

A) Interact often with his rider and try to interact with other horses?

B) Seem focused and attentive, or spooky and reactionary?

C) Appear detached but complacent, or randomly spooky?

D) Seem interactive but testy or threatening?

On a scale of 1 to 10, rate the horse's passive or aggressive behavior.

TURNOUT

When turned out alone, does the horse:

A) Run around calling out and looking for friends, or become very interactive with you?

B) Seem lonely, fearful, or uncomfortable?

C) Let out excess energy and then appear detached or removed from the present situation?

D) Act threatening or aggressive in any way, especially right after he is turned loose?

ASSESSING A HORSE IN TURNOUT

SOCIAL. *Two happy horses contentedly groom each other.*

FEARFUL. *Two horses, each seeking reassurance from the other.*

ALOOF. *These two horses don't interact with each other at all.*

CHALLENGING. *Two horses, fighting for dominance.*

When turned out with another horse, does your prospect:

A) Interact, play, and socialize?

B) Seek reassurance and/or comfort?

C) Ignore or avoid his partner or seem slow to interact?

D) Threaten or try to establish a pecking order?

On a scale of 1 to 10, rate the horse's passive or aggressive behavior.

FEED TIME

When it is time to eat, does your prospect:

A) Call and/or look happy, interested, and welcoming?

B) Seem worried but anticipatory, or fidget or retreat to a corner when you enter with feed?

C) Show a passive or aggressive interest in the food but none in you?

D) Act threatening or territorial about his personal space at feed time?

On a scale of 1 to 10, rate the horse's passive or aggressive behavior.

Mount Up

After you have made mental or physical notes during the first round of observation, the entire process should be repeated with you as the handler or rider. Does the horse act the same with you as he did with his regular handler?

Are his reactions or responses the same but more defined? How do you feel while handling the horse? Do his actions put you at ease, worry you, or threaten you in some way? Pay attention to these important details. They are either the beginnings of your relationship with this horse or good reasons not to start one at all.

YOU & YOUR TRAINER

In a suitable training environment, "good" horses stay good and "bad" horses are repaired. Dreams are fulfilled every day in the horse world by ordinary horses and riders that happen to be in the right hands. There are many talented and hard-working professional horsemen and -women out there — dedicated individuals who truly love horses and are skilled and knowledgeable in their fields. Be sure you have found one of these before you commit to a long-term relationship.

Here are some tips to help guide your journey:

▶ Find someone in your area with a good reputation and then talk to her about how she approaches training.

▶ Look at the horses she is currently working with. Do they seem content, happy, fit, and well cared for? Even if you are not yet knowledgeable, everything the prospective trainer says should make sense and match what you see.

▶ Ask if you may talk to and observe other students during a lesson or watch while horses are schooled. Is each handled as an individual and given a program for success?

▶ Riding and training a horse is humbling work, and any successful horseman knows this. Stay away from know-it-alls.

Analyzing Your Results

First look at the letters you assigned the horse at all the stages of assessment. Here's how to interpret the notes you made.

▶ **Mostly A answers:** Social or Social Mix

▶ **Mostly B answers:** Fearful or Fearful Mix

▶ **Mostly C answers:** Aloof or Aloof Mix

▶ **Mostly D answers:** Challenging or Challenging Mix

If you didn't observe enough clear behaviors to feel confident about your answers, the horse could be very passive or hard to read, or he could be mostly aloof. If your prospect seemed to have responses from many different categories (this rarely happens), then you may have to study him at greater length or get some help from a more experienced observer. If the seller has a solid reputation and knows the horse well, you can show him or her the list and ask for an assessment of the prospect's personality type.

Now look at the numbers from 1 to 10 on the aggressivity scale that you assigned to the horse in each category. The number that appears most often is closest to how passively or aggressively this prospect will express his personality type.

Remember that this is just a first look! Many sellers will not give you the opportunity to look at a sale horse more than once or twice. Pay attention to all of the small details of your interactions with any prospect, and write them down to reflect on later.

Moment of Truth

Now it is time to go back to the earlier chapter that discusses your prospect's type, review the personality information, and ask yourself some questions:

- Have you ever worked with a horse of this personality before?
- If yes, what were the results?
- Does the horse have the proper training for your intended use?
- Is your trainer or instructor comfortable working with this personality type?
- Do you feel comfortable around this horse?

Type vs. Training Issues

One of the most common mistakes made when trying to determine the personality type of a new prospect is to confuse training problems with a horse's personality. A horse that doesn't understand the aids and therefore tunes them out is not an aloof horse; he's a confused one. A horse that is ridden with conflicting aids (for example, reins too strong and nagging legs) may grow angry or resentful; that does not mean he is a challenging type. A horse that is held back and punished may be claustrophobic, but that does not mean he is fearful. A bargey, intrusive horse that is trying to molest you to get a snack may be more greedy and spoiled than he is social. If you suspect there are training or handling issues that are clouding your ability to read your prospect's personality correctly, you will need to step back and think a bit.

Usually in such a situation I put more value on how the horse behaves loose in a field, both alone and with other horses, and how he acts in the stable with a new person, namely you. If his behavior on his own time matches the training issues that you have noticed, then you are most likely witnessing the character of the horse coupled with some training issues. If your prospect is quite a bit different on his own time than he was when being handled or ridden, then I would trust how he interacts and responds in these situations to help you define his type first.

If you are working with a trainer, now is the time to consult him. Can he identify and handle any training issues? Is it worth the investment of time and money to do so?

The Aggressivity Factor

Defining the type of an unknown horse can be difficult, especially if the individual is very passive or you are unskilled at the process. If your subject horse appears to be very passive, displaying very few personality characteristics at all, then personality-wise, you are probably going to be okay. You may still have training or conformation issues to address, but a horse with a number 1 on the aggressivity scale is like a radio with the volume turned down as low as it will go.

A very passive horse of any personality type will have far fewer training issues that are based on character, meaning his character is unlikely to make him behave or "act out" in any significant way. A horse who is higher on the aggressivity scale may need special training considerations based on his loud or more clearly defined personality, just as the overly boisterous child or the classroom bully may need a different sort of handling than would a quieter, more studiously attentive child.

CHAPTER THIRTEEN

YOUR RIDING PERSONALITY

WHICH TYPE OF RIDER ARE YOU? Many new riders have an intuitive idea about their own personality type and what type of horse would appeal to them as a safe but rewarding mount. When tested, however, this intuition often proves inaccurate. Each person's personality and riding type include strengths and weaknesses, so identifying the appropriate personality type in a horse can be much more complex than just analyzing gaits and conformation.

As part of your equestrian journey it is important to realistically evaluate yourself and your riding strengths and weaknesses (and then of course to reevaluate yourself as your skills progress). Once you or your riding instructor have determined the *riding* type that most closely matches your current skill or interest level, you can then work towards determining your basic *personality* type. When you have added your tentative, four-letter personality preferences (and some basic understanding of them) to your riding type, your instructor should then be able to develop a riding program that will suit both your and your equine partner's individual needs.

Self-reflection and self-awareness are important skills to develop and make use of when you are making any life choices. Finding the right horse, instructor, and training program are all opportunities to use these valuable tools.

Defining Your Riding Type

Your current riding type will help define what type of horse you should be riding right now. Your personality type (see page 237) will help define your learning, communication, and decision-making preferences, which will help you in all of your relationships. Awareness of both of these — your current skill level and your personality preferences — will help you decide what type of horse and which riding environment will suit you the best. (See chapter 14 to match horse personality and riding type.)

As you read the descriptions below, you may see the kind of rider you aspire to become. It is important to keep future goals in mind, but first you should determine which profile matches you right now. Your current riding type will be the main criterion to use in deciding which personality of horse should suit you now. As your skills increase, so will your latitude of choices among the four different types and your abilities to deal with more aggressive characters.

It might help to ask your trainer or a riding friend to take an objective look and advise you as to which riding personality is the closest match. An honest and unbiased evaluation is key.

THE ENTHUSIASTIC BEGINNER

These optimistic new riders' knowledge and skill have not yet caught up with their energy or interest. Eager to learn, they apply themselves diligently to their lessons, not letting anything weigh too heavily on them. They may have other interests or hobbies and be trying riding for the first time, or they may be revisiting happy childhood memories. Sometimes riders may stay in this category longer than their skills might indicate just because they haven't yet "thought" about becoming more serious about their riding goals and what the next step might be.

THE CAUTIOUS BEGINNER

These individuals are earnest and sincere beginning riders who seem or may actually be hesitant and/or fearful. Some may have had an unpleasant experience early on, while others may just be apprehensive by nature. These riders want to improve their skills, either to gain confidence or to enjoy their relationship with their horse more fully. These are attentive, yet cautious, students. They do not like to be pushed beyond their comfort level and are slower than others to gain self-confidence, even as their skills increase.

THE CONFIDENT BEGINNER

With no significant worries or fears about riding, these self-confident individuals may have little or no experience but feel they will quickly master any new skills. Some riders in this category may overstate their riding abilities or their accomplishments in order to appear more educated than they are. They may also try to micromanage the details of their riding or horse-shopping experiences, even if not sufficiently informed to do so. They frequently have a controlling or dictating riding and learning style. Mistakes do not bog them down; they tend to "push on," regardless.

THE DREAMER

Meet the idealist, who wants to have a meaningful connection with the entire riding and learning experience. Dreamers may have a tendency to over-personalize horses from their past or present and to believe either the very best or the very worst about all of their experiences. At times they may seem out of touch with the actualities of daily riding and horse management. They may also tend to focus on their riding dreams rather than on how to achieve them with a systematic step-by-step process. They usually want to ride a horse that they feel they can develop an affinity for, both on the ground and under saddle.

THE BACKYARD RIDER

This type is a horse enthusiast who keeps her horses at her own small farm, which was probably bought with that purpose in mind. She doesn't mind the tremendous amount of work that goes into taking care of one or more horses. Her horses are usually pets or companions, and she may not get to ride or pursue riding goals because of time constraints.

If she has not added a riding arena to her establishment, then she probably just likes having horses around and may trail-ride or keep the mounts for absent or visiting family members. Needing a trainer only periodically to help correct a specific riding or handling dilemma, she may be inconsistent about showing up for lessons.

THE HOBBY OR SOCIAL RIDER

The most prevalent type in the industry today, this person enjoys the social aspect of riding and the entire equine atmosphere as much as the riding itself. Often these individuals have not thought about riding goals for themselves and may never get "serious" about their riding. Often they are well rewarded by owning a quality horse that makes a great name for itself even if they are not the rider. This type may often attend clinics, especially with well-known clinicians, but not necessarily to better their own skill level in the way a more serious competitor might. They are usually among the majority of the volunteers that happily participate in making any equine endeavor run more smoothly.

Although hobby or social riders may enjoy showing on a limited basis, it is probably not their main focus. Their primary interest is in safe, healthy fun for both themselves and their horse.

THE ZEALOUS INTERMEDIATE

These riders have had some instruction and acquired some skills but are eager to learn more. They regularly push the boundaries of their riding and showing capacities, wanting to speed up what they often feel is a very time-consuming process. They take an active interest in everything to do with achieving their riding objectives and prefer to learn by doing, not watching. These riders don't mind making mistakes if they think they can learn from them. Often they will apply too much physical energy toward their riding and may need to be reminded not to overstimulate their horse.

THE ACTIVE LEARNER

The active learner is a realistic and self-governed student who understands the basics of riding and that practice makes perfect. These individuals may proceed cautiously when approaching new riding experiences, but they do want to improve and are eager for knowledge. When it comes to competing, they would rather be over-prepared than under-prepared and are usually reserved and humble no matter the outcome.

THE SUPERSTAR

Whether amateur or professional, this is probably a fairly skilled rider (at least in the home environment) who may have enjoyed moderate success in the equine industry. This is not a finished horseman by any means, but he might lead you to believe that he is.

At present he may lack humility, but it will reclaim him should he stay in this business for the long term. In an effort to be the voice of authority, this type may make uninformed decisions or display a lack of necessary objectivity.

THE FOCUSED HORSEMAN

We should all aspire to become or be influenced by this rider, the true horseman. She strives to understand the many factors that lead to an effective horse and rider relationship and never stops trying to improve her methods of learning and teaching. She is attentive to the horse, quietly systematic, and thoughtful in all of her actions. She has a keen, observant eye and the humble sense of humor that many years of hard work can bring. She may or may not enjoy commercial or show-ring success, but her horses respond to her and are happy in their work. There is sound reasoning behind all of her actions, and she is comfortable finding solutions to the inevitable problems that occur in all equine partnerships.

The focused horsewoman may or may not enjoy show-ring success, but her horses respond to her and are happy in their work.

Your Personality Preferences

We have spent much of this book discussing horses' personalities and how our understanding of them can illuminate or predict our equine friends' behavior and responses. Now it is time to focus on our own personalities, an often-neglected but essential aspect of true horsemanship.

Why Study Personality?

The answer is simple and uncomplicated. The primary advantage of understanding your personality type is to enable you to identify your unique gifts. The information you gain will enhance your understanding of yourself, your motivations, your natural strengths, and your potential areas for growth.

Knowledge of type also helps you recognize and appreciate how and why others may differ from you. Knowing that such differences are all valuable and worthy will lead to more constructive communication and relationships.

Lastly, understanding our own type is invaluable in handling confrontations, which occur in everyone's life, be it personal or work-related. Resolving conflict is rarely about who is right; rather, it is an acknowledgment and appreciation of differences.

Understanding Yourself

The best way to examine your own personality is through the Myers-Briggs Type Indicator® (see box). Before you attempt to assess your own type, however, it's important to have a preliminary understanding of the MBTI®, how the eight preferences are defined and recognized, and why it has become such a widely used instrument.

THE MYERS-BRIGGS TYPE INDICATOR

The Myers-Briggs Type Indicator or MBTI® is a personality inventory that was developed by Isabel Briggs Myers and her mother, Katharine C. Briggs. It elaborated on the ideas of Swiss psychologist Carl G. Jung, who endeavored to understand individual differences among people by exploring psychological type.

Myers realized during the 1940s that people could make better career choices if they knew about Jung's types. Consequently she developed the Indicator, refining and revising it over three decades as research was collected on thousands of people.

In all applications of the MBTI®, the emphasis is on understanding valuable differences between people. Knowing "type" not only helps you appreciate your own strengths, gifts, and potential, but also helps you recognize and understand how and why others may differ from you — ranging from your co-workers and friends to your spouse and children.

Now published in thirty languages, the MBTI® is widely used on every continent. Since it's publication, applications of and research on type have exploded. Research has continued to show the relationship between type and careers, intimate relationships, counseling, parenting, children, business, teamwork, leadership, education, and spirituality.

The essence of type theory is that much seemingly random variation in human behavior is actually quite orderly and consistent. This is due to the basic differences in the way individuals perceive life (things, events, people, etc.), and then in how they judge or draw conclusions about what has been perceived. If people differ systematically in what they perceive, and then in how they draw conclusions, it follows that they will differ in their interests, reactions, values, motivations, and skills.

Isabel Myers concluded that an easily administered type indicator could provide a useful way of describing healthy personality differences, and more importantly, that such an assessment could be put to practical use in people's lives. Understanding that the differences among people are all valuable can lead to more constructive and positive communication and relationships.

About Type Preferences

To comprehend personality type, it's necessary to understand type preferences, the basic concept of type theory. Type preferences are innate mental habits, certain consistent differences in how normal people perceive the world. They are best understood as opposite but related ways of using our minds.

Each type preference is indicated by an uppercase letter, and they combine in a four-letter acronym such as INTP. The four sets of preferences (and the letters that signify them) are:

- Extraversion and Introversion (E and I)
- Sensing and Intuition (S and N)
- Thinking and Feeling (T and F)
- Judging and Perceiving (J and P)

TAKE THE MBTI®

I strongly encourage you to learn more about your unique type by seeking out the services of a qualified person who can administer the full questionnaire and share its results with you, including a four-letter type identifier. For more information, contact Gail Rodecker, a qualified MBTI® administrator. See address on the references page.

It is helpful to compare type preference to left- and right-handedness. If you are right-handed or right-hand dominant, you can write with your left hand, but it is usually awkward, unnatural, and slow — probably of poor quality, or childlike and immature. With more effort and time, of course, you could improve the quality of your left-hand writing and become almost as comfortable as with your right or dominant hand.

Our psychological type preferences operate in a similar fashion. When our everyday experience allows us to use our type preferences, we feel confident, competent, and comfortable. But when circumstances require us to use our non-preferences, we may feel less confident, less competent, and unnatural. Quite often, this will cause people to circumvent or avoid situations that call on them to use their non-preferences.

With practice people develop greater skill and confidence in their non-preferences, but due to the time and effort involved, they will typically choose not to engage in behavior that requires the use of their less preferred function. While we all use all of the eight preferences some of the time, each of us has an innate inclination for one of each pair.

Our personality type grows out of our use of our type preferences. There are no good or bad preferences; there are just different tendencies that direct people toward different interests, ways of behaving, and ways of viewing the world. People who have different type preferences also have different strengths, as well as possible areas of needed growth. Acknowledging and understanding these differences lets us appreciate, value, and confirm what each of us brings to the table.

Extraversion and Introversion (E and I)

The first set of preferences, Extraversion and Introversion, are listed first in the four-letter type assessment and are referred to as attitudes. People who prefer Extraversion receive their energy from the outer world of people, things, and/or activities. They interact with the environment, receive energy by actively engaging with people and activities, and acquire new skills through a trial-and-error approach.

Extraverts tend to think best when they are able to talk and interact with others. Spending too much time alone, unable to interact, can cause them to be fatigued or stressed.

People who prefer Introversion receive their energy from the inner world of concepts, ideas, and internal experiences. They will reflect on new ideas and experiences and then determine whether or not to interact with new people or try out new activities.

Introverts tend to think before expressing their thoughts to others and it takes little conscious effort to keep what they are thinking to themselves. In fact, in may be difficult for them to express their thoughts to others without first being able to reflect on them on their own. If they must spend too much time inter-acting with others, and too little time alone, they may become fatigued, drained, or stressed.

Sensing and Intuition (S and N)

The next preference scale, or the second letter of our type, is called our perceiving function: Sensing or Intuition. This determines what we pay attention to or how we understand something.

Sensing types gather information through their five senses. What they notice and trust first are the actual facts and details of a situation. They value information that is practical, with useful applications, and they tend to live in the present.

People with a preference for Intuition look at patterns and relationships to provide meaning to what they perceive. Seeking a general plan or "vision" in a project or endeavor, they may pass over the details. They are more concerned with future possibilities, or what could be, than with the here and now. Intuitive types are more interested in the meaning of information than in the infor-mation itself.

Sensing types sometimes see reality so clearly that they get bogged down in the difficulties of today and miss seeing what's down the road. Intuitive types may get so wrapped up in their visions of what could be that they fail to take the necessary steps to make that dream happen.

Thinking and Feeling (T and F)

How we judge or draw conclusions about the information we take in is called our judging function. Thinking and Feeling make up our third preference scale.

People who have a preference for Thinking tend to look at the logical consequences of a choice or action. They can rather easily take a detached, dispassionate approach to the decision-making process. Sometimes it is only after reaching a Thinking decision that they consider how that decision might personally impact those involved. Often firm-minded, they value logic and truth.

People who prefer Feeling as the basis for their decision-making process take a more personal, connected approach as they look at and consider the data in front of them. Seeking the best decision based on their personally held values, they make every effort to arrive at a conclusion that does not disrupt the harmony and welfare of those affected. Often tenderhearted, they value warmth and compassion.

Both Thinking and Feeling are valid, rational, and reasonable processes. They simply evaluate the information facing them with different criteria: logical principles for the Thinking types and per-sonal values for the Feeling types. It is important to note, however, that as with all the preferences, Thinking types do feel, and Feeling types do think!

Judging and Perceiving (J and P)

The last of the preferences, the Judging-Perceiving scale, deter-mines how you like to deal with the outer world. This letter appears last in the four-letter type assessment.

People with a preference for Judging prefer a structured and orderly lifestyle. Most effective when they can manage and control what is theirs to do so, they like to make a plan and have things settled and decided ahead of schedule. Judging types tend to be task- or goal-oriented, needing closure, sometimes doing so with insufficient data available. (Note that in type language, judging means needing to make decisions, not "judgmental" in the sense of making negative evaluations about people and events.)

Perceiving types prefer a more flexible, spontaneous lifestyle. Curious and adaptable, they like to remain open to new information and experiences and may resist making decisions in order to obtain more data. Sometimes they stay open to new information so long that they miss making important decisions and consequently may miss opportunities.

Summing It Up

Of course, we are much more than just the sum of our four letters. How our four preferences interact with one another, combined with our education, environment, interests, needs, and values, creates the rich and unique individuals that we are. Understanding ourselves and others doesn't sort us into inescapable boxes; rather, it enhances our appreciation of our differences and enables us to find and utilize creative resolutions to our conflicts.

To conclude, it is difficult to know exactly what your type is without taking the MBTI®, and even more difficult to try to guess someone else's type, regardless of how well you know him or her. The potential value — in all your relationships and endeavors — of learning your type is well worth the time, effort, and expense.

TYPE-ING 101

The lists that follow are *not* the Myers-Briggs Indicator, which must be administered by a qualified administrator (see box on page 240). They merely introduce the concepts.

The lists will give a snapshot of what your identifying letters represent. There is so much more to learn about personality preferences that I urge you to explore the great resources that have been published on the subject (see page 290). It's not the purpose of this book to give you a full understanding of all the complexities of type, but rather to ignite your curiosity about personality type in general and your own four-letter preferences in particular. This knowledge will help you in your journey as a rider, and in all of your relationships.

Type Isn't Everything

Type and preference only partly make up who you are. Even though your preferences might be ingrained, as some research suggests, "biology is not destiny." All types behave in varying ways, depending on the situation, the opportunity to learn new skills, and the motivation to do so. Type, in other words, does not imply inherent weakness or strength in any particular attribute. Rather, it indicates, according to the *MBTI® Manual,* that "the preferred starting points for some types may tend to put them at a disadvantage without further intervention, support, or challenge."

EXTRAVERSION (E)

People who have a preference for Extraversion *may:*

- Be energized by other people and external experiences
- Act, then (maybe) reflect
- Be friendly and easy to get to know
- Express thoughts and emotions freely (maybe at risk of saying too much)
- Thrive on interaction
- Give breadth to life
- Appear superficial
- Be absorbed in activities
- Tolerate crowds and noise well
- Seek and enjoy center stage
- Talk faster, and often louder
- Develop ideas and speak at same time
- Have a wide range of acquaintances and friends

INTROVERSION (I)

People who have a preference for Introversion *may:*

- Be energized by inner resources and internal experiences
- Reflect, then (maybe) act
- Be quiet, reserved, and take time to get to know
- Keep thoughts and emotions private (may be at risk of saying too little)
- Need privacy
- Give depth to life
- Seem withdrawn to others
- Be absorbed in thought
- Avoid crowds and seek quiet
- Shun the limelight
- Talk more slowly and usually more quietly
- Develop ideas first and then speak
- Prefer fewer, more intense relationships

SENSING (S)

People who have a preference for Sensing *may:*

- See specific parts and pieces
- Live in the present, enjoying what is now
- Have an eye for facts and details
- Like things that are definite and measurable
- See the details and then the big picture

- Learn new things sequentially, step-by-step
- Have a literal memory for events and conversations
- Trust their experiences
- Tend to be more realistic
- Sometimes focus on the facts of the present or past and miss new possibilities

INTUITION (N)

People who have a preference for Intuition *may:*

- See patterns and relationships
- Live toward the future, seeing what might be
- Have an eye for the abstract and theoretical
- Like opportunities for being inventive
- See the big picture and then the details
- Trust their inspirations

- Learn by jumping in anywhere, leaping over steps
- Have a memory for the general essence of an event or conversation
- Tend to be more idealistic
- Sometimes focus on new possibilities and miss the necessary steps to realization

THINKING (T)

People who have a preference for Thinking *may:*

- Make decisions based on what's most logical first, then its effect on people
- Expect the world to run on logical principles
- Make impersonal judgments, based on objective truth
- Take a long-range view
- Spontaneously critique
- Argue and debate for fun
- Get right to the point
- Excel at analyzing plans

- Seem condescending or distant
- Think with their head, need fairness
- Be more thick-skinned
- Believe truthfulness more important than tactfulness
- Sometimes miss seeing or valuing the "people" part of situations
- Be seen by others as task-oriented, uncaring, and direct

FEELING (F)

People who have a preference for Feeling *may:*

- Make decisions based on what's best for those involved first, and then on what's logical
- Expect the world to recognize individual differences
- Make judgments based on personal values
- Take an immediate and personal view
- Spontaneously appreciate
- Avoid arguments and conflict
- Engage in small talk first

- Excel at understanding people
- Seem overinvolved or emotional
- Think with their heart, need harmony
- Be more thin-skinned
- Believe being tactful more important than the "cold truth"
- Sometimes miss seeing or communicating the "hard truth" of situations
- Be seen by others as idealistic, mushy, or indirect

JUDGING (J)

People who have a preference for Judging *may:*

- Have a planned and orderly lifestyle
- Like their day to be structured and productive
- Like to have life under control
- Enjoy being decisive
- Like clear limits and categories
- Feel comfortable establishing closure
- Handle deadlines, plans in advance
- Seem demanding or rigid to others
- Seem deliberate in their actions
- Be more serious
- Be definite, expressing strong opinions
- Like to set and reach goals
- Often be well organized
- Seek jobs that give them lots of control

PERCEIVING (P)

People who have a preference for Perceiving *may:*

- Have a flexible and adaptable lifestyle
- Like going with the flow
- Like to experience life as it happens
- Enjoy being curious and discovering surprises
- Like freedom to explore without limits
- Feel comfortable maintaining openness
- Meet deadlines by last-minute rush
- Seem disorganized, messy, or irresponsible to others
- Seem spontaneous in their actions
- Be more playful
- Be tentative, reluctant to express opinions
- Be liable to change goals
- Appear to be less organized
- Seek jobs that are fun

As a learner, understanding this concept is key, so that you can make an extra effort to expand the range of tools available to you, whatever your type. For example, Perceivers may need to find ways to ensure they reach completion, and assess their readiness to move on to new challenges, instead of procrastinating. Thinkers might need to work to assess and integrate the unique qualities of their horse into their riding strategy. Extraverts sometimes need to consciously take time to reflect on what they are learning.

Your type preference doesn't mean you lack the capacities represented by the other orientations, but that you *prefer* to rely on those characteristics that come most easily to you. An aware rider can use this information to maximize her personal and professional growth and meet her goals. A person with good "type development" is comfortable with honest self-evaluation and has become reasonably effective in using all of her mental processes as the situation requires. Personality type development or optimal human development is a lifelong process of becoming one's *best* self!

Learning Styles and Type

There is broad agreement in the academic world that a variety of learning styles exists in the general population, beginning in the early years and continuing into adulthood. Clearly, learning goes on long after formal school is completed. There is also no doubt that most competent teachers in any vocation will try to tailor their teaching methods to their students. What is not widely known, though well documented through research, is that our personality type greatly affects how we learn, how we receive information, how we process it, and then how we draw conclusions.

In the world of horses and riding, knowing your own personality type, understanding a little about it, and being able to make necessary adjustments can facilitate and accelerate the entire learning process. Surprisingly few riding instructors/trainers, to date, are aware of the significant advantage of knowing their own type/learning style and that of their students. As a result, they may be unable to address each student in the most appropriate manner and atmosphere. Equally few riders have the self-awareness and knowledge to avail themselves of this invaluable edge.

The sixteen Myers-Briggs Personality Types (the four-letter identifiers) can be grouped in a number of ways. The following method describes, somewhat simplistically, the different ways people approach learning individual tasks. Keep in mind, though, that although type preferences reveal a lot about learning preferences, some learning strategies are independent of one's type.

The four groupings we will discuss are the SF, ST, NF, and NT. Each of these combinations encompasses four of the sixteen Myers-Briggs Types. There are, though, some fundamental differences among the four types in any one group.

For example, of the four SF types (ISFJ, ISFP, ESFJ, and ESFP), two are Introverts and two are Extraverts; two are Judgers and two are Perceivers. The bulk of our mental energy occurs using the S/N and T/F processes. The outside letters (Extraversion/Introversion and Judging/Perceiving) have more bearing on other facets of our behavior and learning capacity. Thus, in relation to learning and teaching styles, grouping the letters in this way is the most straightforward. I will list each two-letter group and then the four Myers-Briggs Types that fall under that grouping.

Sensing-Feeling (SF)

(ISFP, ISFJ, ESFP, ESFJ)

Sensing-Feeling types learn most efficiently when new information is presented in a direct, sequential, step-by-step, fact-based approach, starting with the concrete and moving to the abstract.

▶ They want and need hands-on, useful and practical information, before they want the concepts behind the facts.

▶ In addition to their fact-based learning style, they will perform best in a friendly and warm environment, and need and appreciate positive feedback.

▶ Because they see the present so clearly, they may need help becoming aware of the big picture and visualizing possibilities.

Sensing-Thinking (ST)

(ISTJ, ISTP, ESTJ, ESTP)

Sensing-Thinking types also prefer a sequential, orderly, and fact-based approach to learning that is both reasonable and logical. They want pertinent, precise, and relevant material that they can experience and practice, and then expand to include the general principles and concepts.

▶ They like to analyze and bring natural order out of confusion, with somewhat detached emotional involvement.

▶ They require fair treatment, but may occasionally need to be reminded of the human (warmth) factor that some people must have in order to learn.

▶ Like the SF, they may need help focusing on future possibilities, in order not to get bogged down in the present situation.

Intuitive-Feeling (NF)

(INFP, INFJ, ENFP, ENFJ)

Intuitive-Feeling types learn best when they can explore the general concepts and ideas of a project first. They need to see what a lesson is leading up to, and then they benefit from help filling in the details. Their minds work by skips and jumps, looking for patterns and connections, wherever their inspiration might lead.

- They may be a bit too quick to move on to new skills before honing the present ones.
- They are most capable of visualizing what's down the road with optimism.
- Too many facts and details might stress or bore an NF.
- Of all the types, NFs are the most appreciative of a warm, personal student/instructor relationship, with individual recognition.

Intuitive-Thinking (NT)

(INTJ, INTP, ENTJ, ENTP)

Intuitive-Thinking types like to jump right into new material with gusto. They love nothing better than an intellectual challenge and the freedom to work it out.

- They learn best with logical, organized instructors.
- They appreciate feedback that shows their specific, objective achievement.
- With their focus on the big picture, they may miss out or ignore important details of a situation or issue.
- Because of their firm-minded Thinking function, they might lose sight of the human factor in the learning equation.

Other Influences on Learning

The majority of our mental work is achieved using the two middle letters of our type, called our mental processes, which we have just discussed. The first and last pairs of preferences are called attitudes or orientations. Extraversion/Introversion (how we obtain and expend our energy) and Judging/Perceiving (how we orient ourselves to the outer world) both influence our learning style.

Extraversion and Introversion

Extraverts, by nature, need to interact with their environment, verbally or nonverbally. Introverts, on the other hand, learn by quietly taking in new information and then processing it in their own private, individual ways.

Extraverts tend to "think out loud" or, at the very least, to restate what they think they've heard, as a means of clarifying new information. They like to learn new tasks by talking and doing. Although extraverts can and will quietly focus their attention when necessary, they will be more productive if these periods of serious concentration have regular, active breaks, however brief. They will readily jump into new projects or activities with apparently little consideration, which can be an asset or a hazard depending on the situation. Trainers of young extraverted riders may need to take extra care of their over-eager, over-brave charges. Additionally, extraverted riders need to realize that a lot of learning takes place in a listening or reflective mode (Introversion).

In contrast, Introverts need time to reflect, sort, and study new ideas or details and then, in order to make use of them, see where they fit into their current knowledge base. They may or may not then present their thoughts or work. An Introvert's silence does not necessarily mean agreement or even understanding. Trainers should note that an Introverted rider may not readily express his or her fears, concerns, or questions, and so should act or probe accordingly. Introverted riders need to learn to express their needs and not assume others know exactly what they're thinking.

One could reasonably conclude that many Introverts will need or prefer to be over-prepared for a riding competition (which sometimes holds them back), and that many Extraverts might happily enter the arena somewhat less or under-prepared.

Judging and Perceiving

The Judging-Perceiving preference reveals our work habits and our daily lifestyle. This is directly related to our individual learning style.

Those who have a preference for Judging want a clear work plan and a timely completion of that work. They tend to pursue their work diligently and they want to know how to get from A to B in a precise, timely, and orderly fashion. Therefore, they will want their instruction to be well organized and scheduled. As Judging types take their work and play very seriously, they may need to learn how to lighten up a bit, be more flexible in goal setting, and have more patience with their learning curve. Since Judging types are so focused on closure, they may come to conclusions too quickly, missing some important data.

Perceiving types prefer to experience their learning without a preplanned structure. They are open to varied experiences that go wherever their curiosity takes them. Slow, tedious work is difficult for them as they need their work to feel like play, and they do their best work when they can pursue their problems in their own way. Consequently, Perceiving types may need extra encouragement to plan their riding and training more thoughtfully, especially when leading up to a competition.

In closing, both students and instructors alike could maximize their chances for success by understanding the individual learning styles of the four types and applying them to their specific situations whenever possible.

Gail Rodecker, a qualified MBTI® consultant and long-time rider and horse enthusiast, has contributed the bulk of our type theory information. If you have questions or would like to take the full Myers-Briggs Type Indicator (MBTI®) to become more informed about your individual personality type, you will find her address on the references page.

CHAPTER FOURTEEN

MATCHING HORSE & RIDER

We have come to the all-important question: If I have a basic understanding of equine personalities and have defined my own riding and personality type, *which horse is best for me?* We will discuss general principles first and follow with specifics.

First, though, I must note that we are not talking about the exception to the rule: the person we all at some point have seen taking ridiculous chances on an unsuitable horse and somehow managing to get away with it. That is just ignorance coupled with luck and has no place in a sound riding program. Our goal is to determine the smartest and most productive equine match for our riding and personality type. Whether you are interested in a natural horsemanship project, a finished dressage mount, or anything in between, finding a horse you can get along with is paramount.

Skill level and the right kind of instruction will determine how successfully you can handle a horse as a rider. For those wanting a partner they can bond with and enjoy a relationship with, however, further examination is necessary. Ask yourself: What kind of horse do you admire?

- A brave and fearless horse who will negotiate a hunt field without turning an eye or missing a step? *(Challenging)*

- A timid yet trusting horse who will take confidence from you every step of the way? *(Fearful)*

▶ A lovable lap dog of a horse who is always happy to interact with you? *(Social)*

▶ Or do you just want to get down to business and ride at the barn without all the fluff? *(Aloof)*

Look back at the characteristics of the four different personality types discussed earlier in the book and review some of the case studies. Which relationship can you see yourself in? It is important to remember that it is *you* we are talking about, so be honest about evaluating yourself and consider your own dreams, goals, expectations, and needs.

This book's ongoing refrain has been for you, the rider, to assess the characteristics of yourself, your horse, and your riding situation objectively and observantly. Although some people do get lucky making emotional decisions, in equine matters logical,

TOO MUCH HORSE?

Of course, circumstances may have already put a horse in your life that now, upon reflection, may be more horse than you can handle or make tangible progress with. If that is the case, look at both your short- and long-term goals with this horse and formulate a plan that helps you facilitate them. This plan should include finding a knowledgeable advisor or mentor who is comfortably strong in your weaker areas.

practical choices are the safest and surest bet. If you realize that you are the kind of person who is prone to making more emotional choices, then have your instructor or a riding friend be your voice of reason and practicality.

The Best Horse for Your Skill Level

If you want to ride your new horse immediately, you must first take into account your individual riding type. Your current skill level bears directly on what type of horse you can safely handle, either in an ongoing lesson situation or riding by yourself at home. Here are some pointers.

Beginning and Hesitant Riders

Beginner riders or those lacking in confidence need more passive-social or passive-aloof horses (3 or below on the aggressivity scale) with suitable gaits, training, and conformation for their intended use. A well-trained and very passive-challenging or passive-fearful horse (1 or 2 on the aggressivity scale) may also be suitable, if you have sufficient understanding of the potential challenges ahead and guidance from a competent trainer or instructor.

More Advanced Riders

More seasoned or skilled riders have a bit more latitude in their choices and may enjoy success with horses higher on the aggressivity scale and from any of the four personality types. When the inevitable minor conflicts occur, secure riding skills, competent help, and an ability to understand why your horse might behave in a certain manner should steer you through the rough patches.

The Best Horse for Your Riding Type

Here are some suggestions for the equine personality types that are most suitable for the individual riding types described on pages 232–236. None of this is an absolute science, and if you have a good trainer or instructor who understands both you and your horse very well, you can enjoy much more latitude in your selections.

These recommendations are for the rider of the intended horse. If you will have only an on-the-ground relationship with your horse then you can broaden your selection range, since fewer safety issues come into play when you are not riding.

THE ENTHUSIASTIC BEGINNER

The ideal horse for this rider will be a passively to moderately social or aloof type, with correct conformation and training for the intended discipline. A very passive (1 or 2) mix of any variety could also work, provided you and your trainer are comfortable with the situation.

THE CAUTIOUS BEGINNER

A very passively social horse would be the first choice for this rider, with a very passively social-aloof horse second. A strictly aloof horse (also quite passive) would also be acceptable. Stay away from challenging types or a fearful horse that ranks higher than a 3 on the aggressivity scale.

It is important for this type to ride and learn on a horse who does not have a lot of "training problems" of his own.

PERSONAL PREFERENCE

As a trainer I can handle all different types of horses and do so on a daily basis. If I were choosing a horse for myself based on personality, however, I would lean toward fearful or social types, because I like the attributes they bring to the table. I know myself and my preferences after working with hundreds of horses. As you master new riding skills and improve your ability to ride and handle varying types of personalities, you also may develop clear preferences.

THE CONFIDENT BEGINNER

With the right kind of help and sound knowledge of type, the confident beginner may have success with a passively to moderately social or aloof character and may even enjoy a passively fearful or challenging type.

THE DREAMER

The type of horse this riding type will succeed with depends greatly on their individual skill level. Dreamers tend to be idealistic and can therefore set out to "make things work" with a variety of types. I have found, however, that the best matches are passively to moderately social types and passively fearful types. A social-fearful mix or its counterpart, a fearful-social mix (more passive, 3 or below), is also quite acceptable.

THE BACKYARD RIDER

Because the backyard rider usually assumes all or most of the care-taking responsibilities for her horse, compatibility on the ground is most important. Passively to moderately social and aloof types are the best bet because they tend to cause the least trouble around the barn. Any combination of social and aloof characteristics should also work. These types are also usually the safest choices as backyard riding horses because family members and guests will have the least trouble handling them.

THE HOBBY OR SOCIAL RIDER

These riders may have varying skill levels and expectations regarding what they want from their equine experience, so individual goals need to be factored in. Hobby or social riders of lesser skill need to stay with the more passively social and aloof types. Those with greater skill can choose horses higher on the aggressivity scale and any of the variations in type, provided they have the right kind of guidance.

GREEN RIDERS & GREEN HORSES CLASH

It is very important to remember that the less skilled you are as a rider, the more training your horse should have before you begin riding him. This is true regardless of the personality of your horse or his position on the aggressivity scale.

THE ZEALOUS INTERMEDIATE

Because this rider is usually very goal-oriented, she must select a horse physically capable of helping achieve her goals. Any of the four personality types could be acceptable if the rider has a sound knowledge and understanding of the variations among types, along with a willingness to commit to appropriate training strategies. Keep in mind the differences between similar types that fall at different places on the aggressivity scale and choose a temperament that will help facilitate your riding expectations.

THE ACTIVE LEARNER

Many cautious beginners mature into this type of rider and I would recommend that social horses of passive to moderate range should still be a first consideration. Social or aloof mixes are also acceptable, provided the rider understands enough about type to know which temperament mix he or she has and can factor that information into the training program.

THE SUPERSTAR

This rider probably has the skill and confidence to ride any type so it becomes a matter of choice based on personal preference, goals, and budget restraints.

THE FOCUSED HORSEMAN

This type is likely to be adept at handling any type skillfully but may develop personal preferences over time.

MATCHMAKING BY THE LETTER

If you are a *Thinking Type (T):*

▶ Seek horses that benefit from repetition, such as aloof or challenging horses.

▶ Avoid horses that need social support, such as fearful or aggressively social horses.

If you are a *Feeling Type (F):*

▶ Seek social and fearful horses that love interaction and bond well with their people.

▶ Avoid horses that prefer to be solitary, like aggressively aloof horses, or challenging horses that seem too confrontational.

If you are an *Extravert (E):*

▶ Seek horses that are moderate to aggressive in expressing their personality types, if you have adequate skills. Very passive horses can be overwhelmed by your need for interaction.

▶ Avoid very passive horses, unless you are a beginner, and aggressively aloof horses, because they may be harder to interact with.

If you are an *Introvert (I):*

▶ Seek passively to moderately aloof, social, and fearful types, if you have adequate skills to handle them.

▶ Avoid aggressively social or challenging types. Their constant need for interaction may take you out of your own comfort range too often.

The Best Horse for Your Personality

Below I have listed possible matches for some different personality types. It is important to note that there are so many combinations that could be successful between a horse and a rider, all with varying circumstances, that I cannot list them all. A skillful rider or trainer can make all the difference between success and failure with any horse. If you have realistically evaluated yourself both as a rider and a person, and you have carefully studied your intended horse and his strengths and weaknesses as they pertain to your possible relationship with him, you are on your way to creating a successful partnership.

No relationship is perfect, and any worth having is worth working at. My equine partnerships during the course of my life and career have been very important to me. I therefore took the time to work on them, improving my skills, understanding, and awareness so that I could first understand and then relate to my horses' individual needs.

Working with Personality

As you become familiar with the learning style of your own personality type, you should seek a horse that will be compatible with your particular approach. For example, systematic, step-by-step repetition may need to be tailored or adjusted to encompass the needs of a fearful or challenging horse. The personality types that have most success with challenging types are usually Thinkers in general or Feelers with a high degree of security and skill.

Here are some other cases of horse-rider combinations that are not immediately compatible.

- A cautious or hesitant rider (even if fairly skilled and secure on horseback) may lose precious confidence in the presence of a more aggressively challenging or fearful horse.

- Idealists in particular (NF types), and all Fs to some degree, may become discouraged with a very aloof horse that does not appear to have any desire to bond or interact with them.

- NFs and SFs may also have trouble with a more aggressively challenging horse that seems to thrive on argument.

Those with a T in their personality type may need to work at developing more harmonious and personal relationships with both humans and equines. At the same time, they must understand that for Fs, these types of interactions are more heavily weighted than they might guess.

Those with an F in their personality type may attribute feelings to their horse's actions or behaviors. Unfortunately, very few horses are as emotional as many Fs would like to think. I do know

TYPE IN SHORT

Here is a reminder of the Myers-Briggs Type Indicator® abbreviations.

- I = Introversion
- E = Extraversion
- S = Sensing
- N = Intuition
- T = Thinking
- F = Feeling
- J = Judging
- P = Perceiving

of a few, but they are a very small percentage of the general equine population. Projecting hidden motives onto a horse's behavior usually just muddies the waters.

Quiet, competent, and confident riders, regardless of their personality preferences and choice in equine personalities, may enjoy success with any type, provided they have gained the necessary skills and can understand and remain objective about both training and personality setbacks.

The Best Instructor for You

When you are making the important decision about who can best help and relate to both you and your horse as individuals, a basic understanding of type plays a valuable role. Think back to teachers that inspired you in school. What characteristics did they display that motivated you or facilitated your progress? You will need the same qualities in your riding instructor, *plus* sound, safe, and practical knowledge about your intended discipline.

Some people get lucky and just happen upon someone with whom they click. Others struggle to make sense out of what a trainer or instructor is telling them, afraid to intervene on their own behalf because they feel the issue is their own ignorance and not a basic communication problem between two very different types. I have often noticed, in a variety of disciplines within the horse world, that newcomers think a trainer is a trainer (of course, of course). They don't realize that their learning curve and understanding of the sport would be greatly enhanced if either trainer or student had basic type awareness and a communication style that reflected this awareness.

How KYB Matches Rider and Instructor

My husband, Kim, is an ISTJ (Introverted, Sensing, Thinking Judger). I am an ENTJ (Extraverted, Intuitive, Thinking Judger). Whenever possible, our new students take a personality assessment as part of their orientation.

In the beginning we divide our students, especially novice riders, largely on their Sensing/Intuition preference. We try to put riders who have an S in their type with Kim and the N riders with me. Students who have been riding long enough to acquire basic dressage skills can choose whichever instructor they feel most comfortable with. Over time we will switch so that students receive the same information from a slightly different perspective.

Before we deliberately started this practice, we realized that we had already been dividing our students this way, based just on our interviews with prospective students. I am sure that top teachers and instructors in a variety of disciplines have similar systems.

Many riding facilities, on the other hand, may not normally have two instructors available. In this situation it is helpful if the instructor has a basic knowledge of type, in order to relate to all of his or her students within their comfort level and then help them develop a more diverse perspective.

Neither my husband nor I have an F (Feeling) in our four-letter personality type. This does not suggest that we have no feelings (although I have been accused of such), but it is not our first instinct to factor feelings into our decision-making process. However, in our business and our personal lives we deal with many people who are Feeling types. In order to meet their needs we have both learned to be sensitive to how F types might view a situation.

KYB Dressage's primary function is to develop horses and riders for competitive dressage. Our focus therefore guides our training in that general direction. Consider the overall goals of your riding establishment to be sure that they mesh with yours.

Remember, trainers and instructors are just people. Like everyone, they have a personality, which means they have strengths and weaknesses based on their type and other life circumstances. Here are some of the possible instructor–student combinations.

Extravert–Extravert

If both trainer and rider are Extraverts, then both parties must respect the other's need to have input. The student should defer to the instructor during the lesson. The instructor, however, should allow extraverted students some time for verbal feedback (even if the lesson must end five minutes early to allow this), because that is how they will process information the best.

Introvert–Introvert

If both student and instructor are Introverts, then communication on both sides needs to be practiced and encouraged. The introverted trainer may need to make a special effort to give riders the necessary verbal instruction and feedback. The introverted rider may need to make it a point to ask more questions to ensure proper communication.

Often simply becoming aware of one's own type, strengths, and weaknesses enables us to grow and develop our non-preferences. When Introverts are pressed to use the skills of Extraverts often enough, they cannot help but develop these necessary skills.

Extravert–Introvert

An Extraverted trainer may have to make a special effort to ensure her Introverted student has time for (and is comfortable with) voicing any questions and concerns, since an Introvert keeps much to herself.

Introvert–Extravert

An Introverted trainer of an Extraverted rider should be aware of the latter's need to verbalize as she learns. In turn, this rider may need to be gently reminded that quietly reflecting on new information is very beneficial to the learning process.

Sensor–Intuitive

A Sensing-type instructor will want to explain things in a systematic, step-by-step way. If he has a Sensing student, then everything should be clear. If he has an Intuitive-type student who is not used to gathering information in this manner, they both may feel some frustration. Both should take time to explore the ways their opposite might view and handle new material, as this mental process (our perceiving function) is how we take in information, a crucial component in all riding lessons.

Intuitive–Sensor

Intuitive-type instructors, meanwhile, may speak in metaphors or pictures that are difficult for their Sensing students to follow. They must work at translating their "big picture" ideas into smaller, more usable elements. An Intuitive type must try to look at things from a Sensing perspective. A Sensing-type rider will have to be reminded not to obsess over all the small details, as some things will fall into place at a later time. It will be hard at first: the temptation is strong to keep converting back to your preferred way of handling things whenever aggravation surfaces.

Thinking Type–Feeling Type

A Thinking-type instructor needs to try to weigh the concerns of her Feeling-type student and present information in a manner that is most palatable to the rider. Conversely, Feeling-type students must learn that constructive criticism should not be taken personally or it will impede their learning and progress. Both types need to work towards accepting each other in order to develop more empathetic understanding of any situation.

As an example, a Feeling-type rider may feel inordinately hurt by a judge's seemingly harsh comment on the bottom of a test paper. If she stopped, however, and considered that the judge was most likely a Thinking type, for whom this was a natural way of giving out constructive information, then she need not be upset by the feedback and could instead accept and make use of the advice.

Feeling Type-Thinking Type

A Feeling-type instructor may have her Thinking students wishing she would "get to the point" so real and tangible progress can be made. A Feeling-type will always be more aware of the mood and atmosphere of the lesson than her Thinking-type student requires. Just remember: Thinking types need information.

Judging Type-Perceiving Type

If you are a Judging type, then you like things scheduled, orderly, and on time. This is easy for you because you have honed those skills all your life. What if your instructor or student is a Perceiving type? You may grow annoyed when lessons are repeatedly delayed or put off by someone not so keen on adhering to the time clock.

Before you reach the boiling point, consider that sometimes it is helpful to be more flexible and adaptable. Perceiving types often don't realize that if they run overtime on a lesson or training session it may interfere with someone else's schedule. While it is often true that nothing in the horse world is absolute, and it is best not to be too rigid about your timetable, Judging types often get angry or feel slighted when their timetable is treated casually.

If you are experiencing such problems in your riding environment, communicate your concerns. Explain the differences in your views on scheduling, and ask if your instructor or student might meet you halfway and try to respect your need for a more orderly and cohesive training environment.

This conversation should be just that: a polite discussion between two varying types about reaching a common ground. Conflict or hard feelings need not enter the picture. All self-aware Perceiving types need to learn that the world does indeed run on schedules and keeping to them is very important.

All of these are just examples, and of course there are many variations possible, but you get the point. Everyone is not the same. Understanding a little about type in general, and then your own temperament preferences in particular, will lead you towards more tolerance and acceptance in all of your relationships.

SUCCESS STORIES:
DEFINING PERSONALITY

THE FINAL CHAPTER OF THIS BOOK is devoted to the biographies and personality types of some well-known riders. I am honored that these horsemen and horsewomen agreed to be included in this book. They all took the full Myers-Briggs Type Indicator® and then graciously agreed to share their profiles with you. If your interest leads you in that direction I urge you to do the same. (See the references page for more information.)

Significantly, all of these individuals already pay careful attention to the character and personality of the horses they work with. In part their success is based on either establishing or promoting the individual relationship between horse and rider. Whether they are actually riding the horse, judging at a competition, or producing a possible champion, the notion of partnership, based on understanding individual character, is important to all of these outstanding horsemen.

I hope that the following stories will inform and inspire you, and that you can identify with some of these individuals' characteristics. Furthermore, I hope you will realize that these people have all faced and worked through many of the same challenges you encounter every day of your riding journey. What these individuals did not do is give up or give in to the many roadblocks that are presented to all of us.

ALPHABET SOUP!

For your convenience, here again is a key to the Myers-Briggs® abbreviations.

I = Introversion

E = Extraversion

S = Sensing

N = Intuition

T = Thinking

F = Feeling

J = Judging

P = Perceiving

Here is a key to other abbreviations in this chapter.

AQHA = American Quarter Horse Association

FEI = Fédération Equestre Internationale

MBTI® = Myers-Briggs Type Indicator

NRBC = National Reining Breeders Classic

NRHA = National Reining Horse Association

USDF = United States Dressage Federation

USEF = United States Equestrian Federation

USET = United States Equestrian Team

Dell Hendricks

(REINING HORSES INC.)

Dell Hendricks has an impressive list of credentials. They are both noteworthy and numerous. Highlights include NRHA (National Reining Horse Association) Million Dollar Rider, NRHA Futurity Champion, five-time NRBC (National Reining Breeders Classic) Champion, Multiple AQHA (American Quarter Horse Association) World Champion, two-time NRHA Derby Reserve Champion, and USET (United States Equestrian Team) Team Gold Medalist. Dell has been riding horses since he was a child and is a committed lifelong horseman.

Dell took the MBTI® (Myers-Briggs Type Indicator), and it was determined that he is an ENTP — an Extraverted, Intuitive, Thinking Perceiver. He displays some of the basic characteristics of the ENTP personality type. Many ENTPs have a strong need for achievement, a driving force that Dell is both familiar with and makes good use of. He likes dealing with complex problems and considers the training of each horse as a bit of a puzzle with many pieces that need to be considered and put together just right.

Always one to test new ideas before adopting them, Dell enjoys the process of finding out what works best with each individual horse. He admits that training horses is a wonderful occupation for him because it requires both mental and physical skills. Like many ENTPs, Dell admits that he would not thrive in a job that involved too much repetitive routine, and he is constantly looking for new ways to streamline and improve his process.

Dell is also quick to admit that his training horses are like family to him. One of his favorite horses is Hollywood Vintage (Vinny), the stallion he won the 1999 NRHA Futurity Championship with. He had previously ridden the stallion's dam, Taris Little Vintage, to his first personal major win. He helped foal out Vinny and trained him from the start. Dell prefers to start his own projects, avoiding horses with past training issues whenever possible.

Dell has learned much from the horses in his life. He pays close attention to the personality, intelligence level, and work ethic of all the horses he trains. He is also careful to match up his assistants with horses based on the combination of both the horse's and rider's individual personalities. Although he has had success with horses from all four personality groups, he prefers to work with horses that are overachievers, regardless of type, with a high energy level, even if they are a little more difficult in the beginning. This would suggest horses that are higher on the aggressivity scale of any type.

Preferring training and competing to giving lessons, Dell keeps himself busy doing just that. He has been at USET's Festival of Champions every year since reining has been included. He generally has forty to sixty horses in training at a time and employs three assistant trainers to help with the work. The overall training program, everything from feed to shoeing, is structured and designed by Dell. His wife, Terri, does not ride herself but helps keep his busy training enterprise running smoothly and professionally.

If suggesting a type of horse that Dell might enjoy working with, based on his personality and skill level, I would recommend a social-challenging mix of 5 or more on the aggressivity scale.

Col. Axel Steiner, USAF (Ret.)

FEI "O" JUDGE (DRESSAGE)

The United States has only four "O" judges, and Axel Steiner is one of them. The "O" is the FEI abbreviation for "Official," and all judges at Olympic competitions must hold this license. In many cases the road to judging an Olympic Competition is longer than the road to competing in one and Axel's journey represents a lifetime commitment to the sport.

When Axel took the MBTI® it was determined that he is an ENTJ, a fairly tough-minded personality: an Extraverted, Intuitive, Thinking, Judging type. Axel reflected that his personality has indeed "softened somewhat" over the years. The high rank of colonel, which he earned in the Air Force, is not unusual for someone with his combination of temperament, talent, and willpower, although the title still represents years of dedicated effort.

Axel is typical of the ENTJ in that he is decisive, persuasive, articulate, outspoken, objective, robust, and systematic. Some of the less popular characteristics of this type are arrogance, abrasiveness, and argumentativeness, and Axel admits having struggled with these traits, especially as a young man.

Experience has given Axel a perspective on dressage that few can rival. One of the founders of the U.S. Dressage Federation (USDF), he has since seen it grow to a membership of more than thirty thousand. An accomplished rider in his native Germany, Axel moved at age twenty to the United States, where his talents were quickly noticed. He rode, taught, and competed here as an Event rider until a valuable scholarship offer forced him to give up competition. Since he planned to become an officer, he needed the scholarship, and thereafter his riding changed course.

There still, however, were horses. Axel continued to ride and was noticed enough to be selected as a pentathlon athlete. He admits that, while the riding, shooting, and fencing were right up his alley, he struggled with the swimming and running. Although he did not compete with the team, Axel continued to school the horses, and this led to the beginning of his judging career. Starting with hunter and dressage competitions, Axel eventually officiated primarily at dressage shows, because his interest and passion were there.

When judging, Axel is always looking at the overall picture even as he sums up the parts that need improving. He has an ideal for each level firmly in mind when he is watching any horse and rider combination and a clear standard of what each pair should be able to do. He admits that the small snapshot he sees when someone rides a test in front of him is sometimes not sufficient to pinpoint underlying reasons for mistakes or problems, especially if the rider is skilled in the art of presenting horses. Over time, though, and with more exposure, Axel can confidently point out the strengths and weaknesses of any team.

Harmony between horse and rider is key to Axel, as it should be for any judge. He looks for it and rewards its presence accordingly. Consequently, harsh or unforgiving riders are also noticed and penalized. He feels that at times riders push up the levels too quickly, failing to take the time to perfect the level that they are at in their desire to move onward.

Pivotal to the growth of dressage in this country, Axel is still busy and involved in a variety of activities that lead to the betterment of the sport. He enjoys teaching now more than he used to and likes to observe and promote a good working relationship between horse and rider, whatever the venue. His high standards accompany him from show to show, both around the country and around the world.

Hilda Gurney

(OLYMPIAN, 1976 TEAM BRONZE MEDAL, DRESSAGE)

I could put a list of credentials under Hilda Gurney's name, all of which would be true, and they would not begin to do her justice. A dressage entity, Hilda defies either an accurate and fair description of her personality or a precise evaluation of her talents and achievements. Out of my great respect for all she has accomplished and my admiration for her incredible work ethic I will humbly attempt to do both.

Hilda rode her treasured Thoroughbred Keen to a Team bronze medal at the 1976 Olympics in Montreal. This achievement alone represented years of dedicated work, but she has gained momentum and steam since then. Although widely regarded as one of the pioneers of dressage in this country, Hilda has never been content to rest on her laurels. She remains an accomplished long-term competitor, piloting everything from young horses to finished Grand Prix mounts, most of whom she has trained herself. She is decidedly and refreshingly not "breed-prejudiced," believing and preaching that good horses can be found in many different bloodlines, and she has proven that premise time and again in her own training operation.

An eagle-eyed judge, Hilda looks for the good in every ride but is equally adept at identifying the bad (and deciphering the underlying cause of it) with a skill that few can match. She is known for being strict, clear, and extremely vocal in expressing her many principles. It might be natural to label her as a tough-minded individual, and in many instances that would be correct. Nevertheless, on more than one occasion I have witnessed Hilda take time while she was officiating at a busy show to stop and offer an encouraging word to amateur and junior riders alike.

Central to her accomplishments, or maybe the reason and driving force behind them, is the fact that this remarkable woman simply loves horses. Now what could be better than that?

Hilda took the MBTI® and it was determined she is an ESTJ, an Extraverted, Sensing, Thinking, Judging type. She is typical of the ESTJ in being industrious, dependable, dutiful, tough, outspoken, grounded, and organized.

Even though she agreed to participate in the study, Hilda shared her misgivings about boxing people into four-letter personality groupings. When she answered the many questions on the type indicator, she often felt that both answers for a question would be appropriate, depending on how you viewed them (and that would indeed be a correct assertion). She says that while she may profile as an ESTJ, she does try to have a more diverse approach than her type might indicate when she is handling the various situations and people that surround her in her everyday life. Studies have shown that most healthy individuals do develop their more auxiliary traits as they mature, and Hilda is a prime example of this.

Hilda's work schedule is daunting. On the day we spoke she had started riding at five A.M. and did not finish until after seven that evening. She admitted this was a typical day for her. Most people half her age would not be able to maintain her rigorous timetable for long.

It is important, Hilda believes, to factor the character of the horse into the overall training program. While she may have an idea about a horse's personality after a short introduction, she will continue to study how the horse adjusts and assimilates new information for quite some time.

Although she believes that proper handling, riding, and training will have a definite impact on any horse's ability to perform, regardless of his basic personality, some horses will still have certain associations or behavior patterns, regardless. She related the story of a fine mare that she owned for many years. Although this mare was a wonderful mount who worked well under many different riders when she was on her own property, whenever they took her to a horse show she would fall apart and become almost unrideable. After many attempts to solve the problem Hilda chalked it up to the mare's personality and let her work where she was happiest, which was at home. This mare produced many quality foals for Hilda, none inheriting those fearful tendencies, although Hilda advised that she was careful to select a confident stallion as sire.

Hilda Gurney continues to ride, train, judge, and teach, with no thoughts of slowing her pace. She is a woman to be admired and respected and a force to be reckoned with.

Marcia Smith

(ENDURANCE RIDER)

To condition and train a horse to safely complete a 100-mile endurance test in less than 24 hours is a daunting challenge. To condition, train, understand, and ride so well that you finish ahead of all the other competitors in one of the toughest races in the world — not once, but three times — is almost unheard of.

Marcia Smith is that person. Her accomplishments in the world of endurance racing are extraordinary. At this writing she is the only endurance rider in history to have won the Tevis Cup three times on three different horses. She is also one of only a few riders to have won both the Tevis and the Best Condition award in the Haggin Cup in the same year (1992). She has competed at the World Championships, in 1996 with On A High and in 2000 with Saamson. She has logged more than 7,000 endurance miles, completed over thirty 100-mile competitions, and won the Best Condition award (an exceptional honor) in approximately 25 percent of her races.

I first spoke with her on the phone, knowing her only through her credentials and reputation. I found her interesting, engaging, and articulate, with a refreshingly open-minded curiosity about equine personalities.

Marcia knows the horses that she rides very well. She pays tremendous attention to their basic personalities and uses her understanding of each individual's type to formulate her training program. She has learned firsthand that a horse's athletic abilities are not enough to predict more than his potential in the world of endurance riding. Partnership and the rider's understanding of each horse's individual needs are more critical to success.

Two of the horses on which Marcia had her biggest successes were both problem mounts. On A High was an emotional horse who would internalize his anxieties and often colic during or after races. Marcia's understanding of how to minimize his stress level and handle his anxieties more effectively allowed this horse to reach his potential. Saamson (Marcia's other top horse) had a reputation for being unsafe and dangerous to ride. With time and an understanding of Saamson's insecurities, Marcia developed a potentially difficult mount into an enviable endurance partner.

When Marcia took the MBTI it was determined that she is an ISTJ — an Introverted, Sensing, Thinking, Judging type. Marcia shares many qualities typical of an ISTJ: she is systematic, practical, dependable, precise, articulate, responsible, thorough, and painstaking. She is also skilled at juggling an immense number of facts, a trait common among ISTJs and one that she makes good use of. Marcia must deal with many variables when she designs a conditioning program for herself and her equine athletes.

Marcia competes in a sport that requires a high degree of fitness, partnership, and commitment from both herself and her mounts. She pays close attention to the many important details that must be factored into a successful ride and continually works to streamline her process. She is clearly a caring and committed horsewoman.

My guess is that Marcia has what it takes to work with a fearful-type horse, or a fearful cross, and that horses of these types would find "safe haven" with her.

Tommy Turvey, Jr.

(EQUINE EXTREMIST)

A virtual dynamo, Tommy Turvey, Jr. is an accomplished and skilled trick rider, roman rider, bareback rider (vaulting and standing on the back of a galloping horse), stunt rider, and trick horse trainer. Having performed with horses since the age of eighteen, he is an amazing and versatile athlete whose ability to interact with both his horses and his audience may rival that of the legendary Will Rogers. Appearing comfortable, at ease, and at home performing his many routines in front of large audiences, Tommy makes tricky and dangerous stunt work look no more difficult than a romp in the park.

Tommy has entertained horse enthusiasts all over the world, and his "Riding Instructor" routine (a one-man, one-horse comedy act) is among the very best of its kind, ever. Everything in the act is artfully designed and orchestrated by Tommy himself: the detailed interaction with his horse, the timing and response to his many seamless cues, and the myriad of interactive facial expressions on display. He is skilled with horses in ways few people have ever seen, much less practiced.

When Tommy took the MBTI® it was determined that he is an ENFP — an Extraverted, Intuitive, Feeling, Perceiving type. The ENFP traits that Tommy shares are as follows: he is dynamic, imaginative, expressive, enthusiastic, intuitive, and competitive. Many individuals with his personality type are skilled at improvising, a trait Tommy makes good use of when dealing with new horses, frequent changes of environment, and large crowds. Adaptability is an extremely important asset for any performer and only those who are already familiar with Tommy or his routines would notice when things do not go as planned or rehearsed.

Tommy dislikes too much detailed organization, a trait that is somewhat common among individuals of his personality type. If a situation lacks flexibility or is too humdrum or routine he prefers to delegate it to someone more suited to the task rather than risk putting it off or overlooking it completely.

Skilled at starting horses for a variety of disciplines, Tommy is clever at finding ways for them to enjoy their work. Very few horses will perform the same routines continually if they are unhappy with their training or their handler, and Tommy knows and respects the horses he works with.

He understands the personalities of his horses very well and incorporates this knowledge when formulating a training program for each individual. Most of the horses that he works with in his high-profile routines were originally just backyard horses. They became special and famous because of their training and their relationship with Tommy. His love of both people and animals and his overall zest for life are apparent in every aspect of his business.

Few people in the entertainment business can rival Tommy Turvey as a performer and entertainer. He is a hard-working perfectionist who works daily on improving his relationships with his equine superstars.

I happen to know a few of Tommy's feature horses and therefore can say with certainty that Tommy has had much success with social, challenging, and aloof horses, and their mixes.

Ken Borden, Jr.

(SPORT HORSE BREEDER)

Ken Borden, Jr. is one of the top sport horse breeders in this country. He was the United States Equestrian Federation's Leading Dressage Horse Breeder for 2005. His current stallion Opus is also the number one Breeding Sire in the USEF Rankings for 2005.

Ken's horses consistently rank among the top in this country, year after year. He has either bred, trained, or sold horses that have won at such prestigious events as Dressage at Devon, the Pan American Games, and the North America Young Rider Championships. Two horses he has bred have won a place on an Olympic team — Annetta (for Germany) and Hombre (for Mexico).

Ken has an exceptional ability to choose the right stallion for each mare in his program, based on individual bloodlines, sound knowledge of type and conformation, and a well developed intuition about what each possible match might yield. He is usually right in his choices, and his rather small operation in Wilmington, Illinois, repeatedly turns out horses of a very high quality.

Even before bloodlines, movement, or conformation, Ken pays attention to the temperament and personality of the horses he selects for breeding; in fact, it is number one on his list. Knowing that good temperament will bring buyers back to him tenfold, he looks for it and breeds accordingly. Each year when designing his breeding program, he chooses a few "safe" or proven stallions along with some up-and-coming horses he has a good feeling about. Often he will select one "trendy" stallion to breed to, just for market appeal.

When he believes he has some good prospects he will campaign them extensively, even despite any negative opinions from a few officials, until the horses receive the credit and credentials he feels they deserve. When Ken took the MBTI® it was determined he is an ENFJ — an Extraverted, Intuitive, Feeling, Judging type. The characteristics of the ENFJ type that Ken feels he does share are as follows. He is both easily inspired by and inspiring to others. He is well known in the business for being outgoing, intuitive, expressive, and articulate, all ENFJ traits.

Like many other ENFJs, Ken expects the very best from those around him, and he often finds that these very high expectations yield a very high return. He is hands-on at all times: in fact, he says he is involved almost to a fault and has trouble letting others take the reins from him, even for smaller tasks. Joking that those closest to him often accuse him of being a bit of a control freak, he admits they might not be too far off the mark.

Ken is also a professional actor and college instructor, but both of these careers have taken a back seat to the tremendous amount of energy he has invested in his breeding operation. Although he was originally considered a bit of a risk taker in his breeding choices, his intuition has proven right so often that now others look to him for breeding advice on their mares.

Having spent his life in the horse business, breeding superior sport horses is Ken's ultimate goal. He has led the nation in producing great Appaloosas, Quarter Horses, and Arabians and is now one of the top sport horse breeders in North America. His legacy will continue to grow for years to come through the quality of the hoof prints his horses are leaving in the sand.

CONCLUSION

THE OLDER I GET, THE MORE I REALIZE that all of life is about connecting on some level or another. The connection with family and friends. The connection with those in your work or school environment and those in your social strata.

Connection is one of the things we enjoy most about our pets, be they dog, cat, or horse. I have learned to connect with horses because I have been interested in their behavior for many years. I have learned to connect with people because I have become motivated to do so.

I hope that this book has given you a basic awareness of the differences in equine personalities and ignited some curiosity about temperament in general, improving all your relationships through better understanding. This awareness may indeed be the missing link you have searched for in your riding, and if so, your riding will improve because of it.

Horses are magical, wonderful creatures and this book is not designed to dampen the imagination of any horse enthusiast by taking the excitement out of building your equine partnerships. My intention instead is to help you realize that every horse behaves as it does for many tangible reasons. If I have succeeded, you will better understand equine personality type and how to define it accurately by observing actions and behaviors.

I have enjoyed writing this book for many reasons and on many levels. This process has allowed me to re-visit some of my treasured equine friends. It has reminded me to approach new people and new horses with respect but also with curiosity. And I have confirmed to myself that all behaviors are clues that, with an investment of interest and time, help us to more accurately define and understand the whole picture of a personality.

In closing, I must point out something that was not easy for me to learn but may be the most vital message I can share on this subject. There is no one type (either human or equine) that is better than the others. Different strengths, different weaknesses, certainly, but not better and worse. I have learned over the years that some horses are more suited to certain activities than others and that certain individuals will be more skilled at handling and presenting them. Having stated that, however, I also realize that with the right amount of time, interest, and willingness to acquire necessary skills, anything and everything is possible.

Happy riding and good luck in all your equine endeavors!

— Yvonne Barteau

REFERENCES

Lawrence, G. 2000. *People Types & Tiger Stripes.* Gainesville, FL: Center for Applications of Psychological Type, Inc.

Martin, C. 1997. *Looking at Type: The Fundamentals.* Gainesville, FL: Center for Applications of Psychological Type, Inc.

Myers, K. and Kirby, L. 1994. *Introduction to Type Dynamics and Development. Exploring the Next Level of Type.* Palo Alto, CA. Center for Psychologists Press, Inc.

Myers, I. with P. Myers. 1995. *Gifts Differing.* Palo Alto, CA: Consulting Psychologists Press, Inc.

Myers, I., McCaulley, Mary H., Quenk, Naomi L., and Hammer, Allen L. 2003. *MBTI Manual.* Palo Alto, CA: Consulting Psychologists Press, Inc.

Quenk, N. 2000. *In the Grip: Understanding Type, Stress and the Inferior Function.* Palo Alto, CA: Consulting Psychologists Press, Inc.

VanSant, S. 2003. *Wired for Conflict.* Gainesville, FL: Center for Applications of Psychological Type, Inc.

Gail Rodecker, certified Myers-Briggs consultant: mbtirodecker@sbcglobal.net.

Visit Yvonne Barteau's Web site at www.kybdressage.com.

GLOSSARY

AT LIBERTY. The art of working a horse loose in the arena, having him respond to whip signals and body language in order to obey.

BEHIND THE LEG. Describes when a horse does not move freely forward from light leg pressure. He may feel sluggish or tight and not respond to leg aids in general. A variation is to be tight and stiff and overreact to leg aids without accepting the leg pressure.

BERM. An earthwork around the perimeter of an arena.

BOLT. Run off at high speed, seemingly blind and oblivious to the surroundings.

COLD-BACKED. Describes when a horse is very tight in the back during saddling or mounting. The condition may cause the horse to buck, rear, run off, or fall down.

COME OFF THE AIDS. Stop responding to the rider's signals.

CRIBBING. An equine bad habit, involving grasping a solid object (such as a door) with the teeth and sucking in air.

DISASSOCIATING. Deliberately ignoring what is happening to one.

DRESSAGE SCALE. A training guide for dressage, in which each step, once gained and mastered, leads naturally toward the next. The dressage scale was developed by the German cavalry in 1912 and is still used worldwide. (See box on levels, next page.)

FEI. Fédération Equestre Internationale (International Equestrian Federation), the governing body of international equestrian sport.

GOING TO THE BIT. When a horse actively seeks contact with the hand by stretching toward the bit and then maintains contact because of this desire.

GRAND PRIX. The highest level of dressage competition.

GREEN-BROKE. Started and comfortable with a rider but not yet trained.

HAND-GALLOPING. Letting a horse gallop (which is faster than a canter), but keeping him controlled and not at top speed.

THE DRESSAGE JOURNEY

Dressage tests are divided into levels that introduce progressive challenges, as follows:

INTRODUCTORY LEVEL	Two tests and two gaits, the walk and the trot.
TRAINING LEVEL	Four different tests introducing patterns requiring basic working walk, trot, and canter.
FIRST LEVEL	Four tests adding leg-yielding and lengthening of the stride at both trot and canter.
SECOND LEVEL	Four tests, introducing more lateral exercises (collection, shoulder in, and haunches in) and turns on the haunches in walk.
THIRD LEVEL	Three tests adding extended trot and canter along with flying changes at the canter and more lateral work (half-passes).
FOURTH LEVEL	Introduces sequence lead changes every three and four strides and half pirouettes in the canter.

Next come the FEI tests (International Equestrian Federation), as follows:

PRIX ST. GEORGES	Requirements similar to the Fourth Level with a higher degree of proficiency expected from horse and rider.
INTERMEDIATE TWO	Adds full pirouettes and lead changes every two strides.
INTERMEDIATE THREE	Introduces the wonderful floating trot (Passage) and on-the-spot trotting in place (Piaffe), along with lead changes each and every stride (the horse looks like he is skipping). This is the level at which Olympians compete.

Scores are given for each required movement in a test and the total score is then made into a percentage score. Low 60s are average scores, especially as you move higher up the levels. Mid- to upper 60s and anything in the 70s is quite good.

HIGH-SCHOOL LEVEL. A level of dressage training that includes high-school movements ranging from "airs above the ground" to "Spanish walk and trot" or piaffe and passage.

HIT-AND-HURRY JUMPING. A jumping round that counts only time and faults.

JUMPING IT OFF. A racetrack term for when a Standardbred quits trying on purpose, deliberately breaking out of the trot or pace gait into a gallop.

LONG. Late into a racing season.

NAGGING. Repeatedly applying the same aid at the same level of intensity.

ON THE BIT. Describes when a horse stays connected to the hand through impulsion and acceptance of contact.

OVERFACING. Asking a horse to do more than he is physically or mentally capable of at the time.

PASSAGE. A highly elevated trot with a distinct moment of suspension.

PIAFFE. A trot in place during which the horse maintains a clear rhythm and lifts diagonal pairs of legs while maintaining contact and self carriage.

PONYING. Leading one horse while riding another.

ROUND AND DEEP. Describes when the poll of the horse is lower than the withers and the nose is behind the vertical so that the back comes up a bit rounder than normal. The horse is still lightly connected to and going toward the bit and should always be ahead of the leg in this work.

SET [HIM] DOWN. Put in [his] place, as in the pecking order.

SPOOKING. Shying or having a startled reaction, sometimes out of actual fear and sometimes as a way to come off the aids of the rider.

TEST (DRESSAGE). See box, opposite page.

VETTING. An examination of a horse by a veterinarian, which may include x-rays to determine soundness for purchase. Also known as a pre-purchase exam.

WASHING OUT. Sweating profusely in nervous anticipation of a race or any experience that causes a horse anxiety.

INDEX

Page numbers in *italic* indicate illustrations or photographs; those in **bold** indicate tables.

Other Storey Titles You Will Enjoy

101 Dressage Exercises for Horse & Rider,
BY JEC ARISTOTLE BALLOU.
Fully diagrammed standard dressage techniques to create a firm
foundation for all performance riding.
240 pages. Paper with comb binding. ISBN-13: 978-1-58017-595-1.

How to Think Like a Horse, BY CHERRY HILL.
Detailed discussions of how horses think, learn, respond to stimuli,
and interpret human behavior — an illumination of the equine mind.
192 pages. Paper. ISBN-13: 978-1-58017-835-8.
Hardcover. ISBN-13: 978-1-58017-836-5.

The Rider's Problem Solver, BY JESSICA JAHIEL.
Answers to problems familiar to riders of all levels and styles, written
by a clinician and equine behavior expert.
384 pages. Paper. ISBN-13: 978-1-58017-838-9.
Hardcover. ISBN-13: 978-1-58017-839-6.

Storey's Guide to Training Horses, BY HEATHER SMITH THOMAS.
Vital information about the training process, written from the stand-
point that each horse is unique and needs to learn at his own pace.
512 pages. Paper. ISBN-13: 978-1-58017-467-1.
Hardcover. ISBN-13: 978-1-58017-468-8.

Storey's Horse-Lover's Encyclopedia, EDITED BY DEBORAH BURNS.
A user-friendly, A-to-Z guide to all things equine, including line
drawings, lists, diagrams, and helpful tips.
484 pages. Paper. ISBN-13: 978-1-58017-317-9.

Storey's Illustrated Guide to 96 Horse Breeds of North America,
BY JUDITH DUTSON.
A comprehensive encyclopedia filled with full-color photography and
in-depth profiles on the 96 horse breeds that call North America home.
416 pages. Paper. ISBN-13: 978-1-58017-612-5.
Hardcover with jacket. ISBN-13: 978-1-58017-613-2.

These and other books from Storey Publishing are available
wherever quality books are sold or by calling 1-800-441-5700.
Visit us at *www.storey.com*.